EBURY PRESS

BUILD, DON'T TALK

Raj Shamani is the founder of House of X, an entrepreneur, a podcaster with 100 million views, a keynote speaker who has given speeches in twenty-six countries and a social media content creator with more than 2 million followers. His podcast, *Figuring Out*, is the top podcast on entrepreneurship in the country. He is one of the youngest Indians to have spoken at the United Nations. He has been featured in *Forbes* ('Top 100 Digital Stars in India'), YourStory ('Top 5 Young Influencers of India') and *Asian Age* ('Top 10 Young Entrepreneurs in India').

Build Don't Talk

Things You Wish You Were Taught in School

RAJ SHAMANI

EBURY
PRESS

An imprint of Penguin Random House

EBURY PRESS

USA | Canada | UK | Ireland | Australia
New Zealand | India | South Africa | China

Ebury Press is part of the Penguin Random House group of companies
whose addresses can be found at global.penguinrandomhouse.com

Published by Penguin Random House India Pvt. Ltd
4th Floor, Capital Tower 1, MG Road,
Gurugram 122 002, Haryana, India

First published in Ebury Press by Penguin Random House India 2022

ISBN 9780143459682

Typeset in Sabon by Manipal Technologies Limited, Manipal

www.penguin.co.in

Contents

Fact: Most people don't achieve anything in their life because most people don't do anything in their life. If you belong to the number who will say, 'I will read the first chapter tomorrow', put this book down. Forget the book. I don't want you to read this book. If you're going to read a chapter a day, only then read the next line. You are starting a new life with this book. This book can be completely useless or completely valuable for you; it's up to you to decide.

Preface: Little Accomplishments

I hate reading books, but I'm writing one.

If you love reading books, read away. If you hate reading, then go watch my videos or listen to my podcast because there's no one way of learning. There is only one way of growing though, and that is through little accomplishments.

Life is all about little accomplishments. I don't want you to read the whole book right away; I want you to read this one chapter, that's it. Put this book down if you want to finish reading this book in one go. Frankly, I don't want you to complete this book. I don't want you to take away anything from it apart from the fact that you have to finish one chapter a day. That's it.

It's hard to form good habits, even harder to stick to them. When we look at a project as a whole, we see how much we have to do, and it becomes burdensome. Take this book for instance. Writing 50,000 words? Oh, God! I'm panicking even at the idea.

I don't know how to fill so many pages! I'm legit staring at my laptop screen, typing these sentences and trying to figure out if it makes any sense. But then again, I'm doing it one sentence at a time, one paragraph at a time, one chapter at a time. And soon enough this book will be in your hands and I'd have done my job.

Writing a book is uncomfortable. Getting out of our beds in the morning is uncomfortable. Attending that online class where you have no idea what the tutor is teaching is uncomfortable. Going to that job that you absolutely hate is uncomfortable. Executing all those plans that you have been making, or let's say daydreaming about, is uncomfortable. They are all uncomfortable. But just because something is uncomfortable doesn't mean you stop doing it. Growth is uncomfortable, but being uncomfortable is the only way you grow.

If you're thinking, 'But Raj, I just don't think I can do it today. I want to give my best', then you need to accept that there are going to be days when you won't be able to give your best, and that's completely okay. Sometimes trying is all you need to do. Sometimes, showing up is the most you can do.

This is the reason I don't want you to finish this book in a day, because I didn't write it in a day. Ever heard that phrase, 'Rome wasn't built in a day'? One brick at a time, one sentence at a time, and one chapter at a time, that is how we are going to do this.

If you do that, that's a win for me. Complete one chapter a day so that you are building small habits and you're achieving small things every day. That's a good habit to inculcate in your life: little accomplishments every day, consistently.

1

Our Education System Sucks!

Imagination and emotion are the only two blessings human beings have, which the education system is killing from day one.

There are three types of learners: auditory, visual and kinaesthetic. Auditory learners learn through talking and listening, visual people learn through looking at things and reading things, and kinaesthetic people learn through experience. Every single person is partially kinaesthetic, because everyone learns best through experience. I've given more speeches after getting inspired by a music album than I have by reading books.

The problem with traditional education is that we are taught 'what to learn', but we are not taught 'how to apply'.

We are taught to read and study a subject, but the first step of an education system should be to help people discover themselves and the way they learn best. Nobody teaches us *how* to learn, though, and what is the best way we can learn.

Since day one, each one of us is a different human being. We are brought up differently, we have different senses, the way we perceive the world is different, we are born and brought up in a different kind of environment, we have different talents, skills and abilities.

You might learn from watching videos, I might learn by reading a book, somebody else might learn through experience, by actually doing things. An education system should be focused on helping us to explore what the right way to learn is for us, so that we know from the very beginning that this is the way I, as an individual, learn the best. But, currently, everybody is taught to learn the same thing in the same way. What if I'm a video person? What if I'm a kinaesthetic person? You are telling me to read, cram and then write what I remember. Reading is amazing, but what if somebody is not a reading person? The education system should be designed to help us explore our best learning form because only then can we accelerate our learning process and thrive. If you know you learn through reading books, then you can order twenty books, read them and get ahead. If I know I learn through watching videos, I can watch a hundred videos in a year and get ahead of the current 10+2 education system. If I know I learn best after talking to people, I can arrange meetings across the world and get ahead of the 10+2 system in just six months.

By the time we go to college and enter the brutal real world, a dynamic world where everything happens in a second, we would want to learn anything and everything in our lives and get ahead. But that is the time when we actually start to learn what our medium is.

Another issue I have with education in school is not the content—it is that we are not taught how to use that content. We are not taught to think, we are taught to memorize and write. Whatever we are taking in, without ever processing it, we have to take it out. They have made human beings a simple printer, not even an intelligent printer. We should be machines who can think and perceive things emotionally. Imagination and emotion are the only two blessings human beings have, which the education system is killing from day one. We are not taught to imagine, be curious, ask questions, think. We are not encouraged to challenge the status quo. If we are not taught and encouraged to do this, how will we ever learn how to challenge and take the human race forward? That's why most people who are high achievers or high performers are not very well educated. They are obsessed with one thing, they are the best at the one thing that they do, but they are not well educated.

There is one thing which I say a lot: 'People who study a lot often study about people who do not study at all.'

If I open a school, I would like to make it the exact replica of reality. In the real world, everyone tries to sell everything to everyone. If you're a doctor, you're selling drugs. If you're a content creator, you're selling your content. If you're a writer, you're selling your articles. Everyone is selling themselves or their services or their products. What I would do is, at the start of every year in school, all the children would be given a business and told to make it grow. We would help kids monetize it in their break, and they would be taught how to negotiate, how to talk, how to sell, how to not sell. This way, they will learn that people sell and do everything possible to make their business grow to get ahead in life; it's not only about marks. In my school, everybody would get a platform to learn communication, learn negotiation, learn selling, learn how to source things, to sell things, how to identify the target audience. They would learn whom to hang out with, whom not to hang out with. They would learn to identify who is a potential paying customer and who is going to turn into a bad debt. They will basically understand people, understand themselves, understand their business model, understand sourcing and selling—all of it just in a small short break.

Most schools organize annual functions, for which students are supposed to make projects; they create and showcase a product. *Life mein ek bar har cheez ko event jaisa bana diya*—that is not going to work in real life. Exhibitions are nonsense. Real life is not an exhibition, real life is real-time hardcore selling. It's not like you are going to think of something for one month and exhibit it in front of people and everyone is going to applaud. Let's give kids an understanding of money transactions. Let's give them an understanding of give-and-take relationships. Let's give them an understanding of people. In reality, it's not about exhibiting one time a year; in real life it's about making decisions and changing constantly on a daily basis so that you adapt and win in life. If you start establishing that in ten-minute short breaks, everyone can do their business, and based on that they are going to get assessed in life. Boom—a daily business can literally take the entire country forward. Because everybody would have a deep understanding of what they like, what kind of customers they want to target, what is their product and how they can improve that product; how they can source, how they can tax, how they can do everything possible on a daily basis in ten minutes. These ten minutes over a long time compound into one big useful thing—instead of doing one project for one day for an exhibition, and then just forgetting about it.

The pace at which Israel is growing and the way its people have taken their country forward is phenomenal. No other country is growing at this pace. One of the major reasons is that Israelis are taught to think and ask questions. Indians are taught to stay dumb. When we ask stupid questions, people ask us to shut up and laugh at us. In Israel, when a kid comes back from school, their mother asks them which was the best question that they asked today. Children, having the tendency to please their mothers, make it a point to ask questions in school. Now, every day, the kid is thinking about asking one question to somebody, so the mother is impressed. The kid is taught to ask questions every day. How beautiful is that? This simple task fuels curiosity in kids and makes them ask more and more questions. This is something which I think every parent should adopt. It creates better individuals for the future. That's how the human race moves forward.

Our education system sucks! We should focus on questions, curiosity and appreciation. In my head, in the perfect school, every time someone asks a question, they will be told 'you are curious', not 'you are stupid'. No question is stupid, it's just a way of seeing things. Something which is stupid to me is not stupid to you, and vice versa. Why do some people in school have the right to decide whether or not my questions are stupid? How can they dismiss me and my curiosity?

In our current education system, when a kid scores ninety out of 100 in English and forty in maths, they are asked to take extra classes and focus on maths, instead of being told they are doing great in English, and that they could have an amazing career in writing or something similar. We discriminate between subjects, saying one is more important than the other, and on the basis of that we decide whether a student is intelligent or not. A kid scores well in maths? They are very bright. A kid scores well in English and not in maths, they are regarded as useless. Our school system doesn't focus on our strengths; instead, it ridicules us for our weaknesses.

No two students are alike, and we need to mould our education system in a way that embraces each student's individuality. In an ideal school, if a student is good at something, they would be encouraged to do more of that thing, meet more people from that field, explore the things they can do in that area, and be motivated to pursue what they like, instead of following the herd and doing engineering.

Schools give us a certificate of participation, *but life mein ghanta milta hai participation ka*. In life, you either win or you lose. Nobody is going to hand you a candy in the real world, saying, 'Oh, my God! You participated!

Here, take a part of the profits too.' No! You either get the business deal or you don't. Investors won't put money in your business just because you were present in a room full of start-ups.

I don't understand equality. Life is not equal. Life is brutal. I think if, as kids, everybody was made to understand that the world is an unfair place, the way we live and the way we think would be so much better. Because of two things: number one, you know the world will trample you the first chance it gets, so you will always be prepared and work harder. Number two, you will always try to make this world a better place because it is a brutal world. But no, we are taught the opposite. We are taught that this world is a fairyland. That's why we never try to make the world a better place. We think, 'Oh, maybe there is something wrong with me or the people around me are stupid.' We think that if only we could get out of this current place and be around different people, things would be better. So you move to a bigger city, only to realize that people here are worse. And then you never settle because you are trying to find somebody better somewhere, some place that is the fairyland that we have been told about.

Now, imagine if we were taught that the world is a brutal place, and we were put together with five people that we know. Now, all of us know that life is tough, and everybody is going to live for themselves. You and your group of five would come together and try to create something beautiful. Instead of finding that peace with somebody else, we will try to correct the person who is with us. And that's how you build a better human network.

My perfect school would be an immersive learning experience. One month of studying in the mountains, and the next month we would be on the road. The month after that we would be on a beach. We learn so much more through experiences than we would ever do from textbooks. And that is what we need to promote.

But until I build the school of my dreams, I am going to try to teach everything I believe in, everything that I have learnt, through this book. So, until that school is created, read away.

Key Takeaways

1. Know how you learn.
2. Be curious—ask questions.
3. You don't get a certificate of participation in real life.
4. Life is not fair, it is brutal.
5. Create better human networks.

2

You Suck—Admit It!

*Until we admit that we suck at things, we won't be
able to work on the part that sucks, and our ego
won't let us grow.*

Before actually getting into the book, let me tell you
this one thing—you suck. You suck more if you think
you don't suck. That's the harsh reality. And the
harsher reality? The person who will tell you to admit
you suck won't accept that they suck too. But I'm
admitting it—I suck!

I suck at so many things. But how do I know I suck
at them? Because I've tried them. I realized I suck at
sports because I tried. I realized I'm musically challenged
because I tried. You can't just do nothing on the excuse
that you suck. Because in that case, it will be just that—
an excuse.

There are people in this world who don't try anything
with the excuse that they are bad at it. Others start
something, know they suck at it, but don't let go of it

because of some false sense of superiority. Being in either one of these groups is stupid. You wouldn't want to suck and be stupid at the same time, would you? If you belong to the first category, you're self-criticising without even giving yourself a fair chance. If you are so critical of yourself, what will other people do? You have heard that song, *Kuchh toh log kahenge, logon ka kaam hai kehna*, right? So, let the *log* say, no?

And if you belong to the second category, that is, remaining stuck at something when you know you are bad at it and yet not ready to let go, let me tell you, you're even more stupid. Be it a course, a relationship, or a job, when it's not working, it's just not working. You need to admit the fact instead of trying to fight the obvious.

Do you remember a time in school when you went on stage and completely forgot what you were about to say? I remember it happening to me. I was supposed to read the generic thought of the day on stage. I went up on stage and started, 'My name is Raj Shamani and this is the thought of the day . . .' And then . . . blank! I completely forgot what I had to say.

We all have a similar story from our lives that we remember and laugh at. But what we did after that situation, whether we left it at that or worked hard to improve it, is what makes the actual difference. I realized I sucked at public speaking. Considering I am a public speaker now, you can imagine the hustle that would have gone into it.

The world is so, so big and so are the opportunities. You can only avail the opportunities if you know your capabilities along with your weaknesses. Acknowledge your weakness and overcome it with the help of your capabilities. It's basic SWOT analysis.

For me, I know I suck at writing and how did I get to know that? By trying it first. And I absolutely sucked! Then how am I writing this book, you ask? Simple: I hired a ghostwriter to write this book for me. Because, at the end of the day, I just want my thoughts to reach you—I don't care who is writing them down. And you're not going to bother about who wrote the book; you are just going to care how this book helped you. So, I am admitting that I suck at writing, which is why I hired professional help.

And that's your solution right there. If you suck at something, admit it. But don't just stop at that. Because what you do about it is what makes the real difference.

Most people feel bad about admitting that they suck at a particular thing. In fact, the first step towards growth is to understand that we suck at certain things and that it is completely okay.

I have sucked at a lot of things all through my life and you will get to know about them as you read the book. Sucking at things has always been a constant. But the second constant has been how I overcome it.

I try something, I realize I suck at it, I analyse how crucial that thing is for my growth. If it's important, I try to get better at it. If I get better at it, then great! I can go ahead with my life and find the next thing that I suck at and try to improve on that.

But if it is something important and I can't get better at it even after trying, then I do what I did for this book: get a professional to do it for me.

Now coming to the second part of this whole scenario, being stuck at something even when you know you are bad at it. It is important to improve, but the other thing as important as improving is knowing when to quit.

Again, we will talk about 'quitting' in more detail later in this book, but for now, if something is not working out for you, quit. Life is too short and there are too many other opportunities to be stuck at a thing that is not working out.

So, how is this whole admitting-that-you-suck-thing going to work out for you? Let me explain.

You admitted you suck, and you left it at that. Are you ever going to grow with that approach?

NO.

On the other hand, you realized you suck at something and asked yourself whether you can get better at it. And how you can get better at it.

Now that will make the difference.

If you think you can get better at it, research and learn and get better. If you think you can't do it, take professional help and find someone who can do it for you. But don't let it stop you from growing.

This is the lesson we need to learn. We realize and accept that we're bad at something. And we either work on that aspect ourselves, or we find someone else to do it for us.

If there is only one lesson that you take from this book, then let it be this: admitting that you suck.

Key Takeaways

1. There are things you suck at, accept that.
2. Learn and get better at the things you suck at.
3. Stop making excuses, start taking action.
4. Know your capabilities and weaknesses.
5. It's okay to quit.

3

Jack of All Trades, Master of None

Life is like a buffet; get up and pick what you want. Try looking at, smelling and eating different things, and then take more of what you like. Don't treat it like an à la carte, because no one is going to serve you your favourite dish on the table.

Fortunately, or unfortunately, I was born in a family of toppers. All my cousins were toppers and everyone would tell me to study. Or else, they said, while they would become engineers and doctors, I'd end up as the peon outside their office. Three of my cousins were in the same class as me. And they'd all score 95 per cent, 94 per cent, 93 per cent—while I got 43 per cent. I always had this constant pressure that I had to do better, or else I would be humiliated in my own house.

All through my school years, I was branded as a useless kid. So much so that even my parents didn't give me the usual doctor–engineer options while I was growing up. My father wanted me to be either an actor or a sportsman. Lucky me! Eventually, I also thought since nothing great was happening with my studies, let's try sports. I tried basketball, but I was too short to play. I tried football for the next six months and broke my leg while kicking the ball. I started playing table tennis, but found it too boring. I kept bouncing from sport to sport until I figured out there was no way I could have a career in sports. (The positive side? I know how to play all of them.)

On top of all this, my classmates were like, 'Oh! You can't speak English? You can't sit with us.' And I felt . . . I felt inferior.

Like every other self-conscious kid, I wanted to be cool. In eighth standard, I started listening to Linkin Park because that was the only way I could learn English. So, I went on Google, searched for the lyrics and sang along with a song until I knew all the words. I went to school and started singing in front of my class. My classmates flipped. 'Raj has such a good command over the language.' '*Raj toh English me itna fast gaa raha hai, Raj toh bahot cool hai.*' (Raj is singing so fast in English, he's so cool.)

I was like, okay, I'm going to become a rapper. So, I wrote some stuff and rapped it without any music. They all told me, 'Raj, let it be.' It was so bad that even I didn't listen to it twice.

So, what's next, I wondered. How can I become cool? Well, every movie that I watched told me that if I wanted to be cool, I needed to learn how to play the guitar. And that's what I did. So, in ninth standard, I started learning how to play the guitar and realized that it's not as easy as it looks. Your fingers hurt like hell.

I had a new career option every year because the first career option—studying—was not working out.

In tenth standard, I decided I would be a DJ. 'DJing is just 4x4 beats, it will be really easy,' I thought. Now, I wanted to be Hardwell, all of a sudden. I tried that for a while but couldn't get anywhere with it. Let's just say I was musically fascinated but I was musically challenged.

While DJing, I realized that in the entire one hour at the console, my favourite part was screaming 'Everybody jump!' I didn't have any interest in the music, this was the only part that I loved. So, once I had this realization, I moved on.

Then, in eleventh standard, a movie called *Zindagi Na Milegi Dobara* was released, and I thought, okay, I want a house in London like Hrithik Roshan. I decided to become a financial trader. I learnt about stocks, made a dummy portfolio, and after eight months I found out I'd lost money. I realized I was not good with numbers. I thought I was earning a profit but I ended up with a loss. 'Boss, this is not for me,' I told myself.

By the end of eleventh standard, I was back to square one. I became that lazy kid again. I left all the hustle and told myself we'd see what would happen, how things would turn out. I just wanted to chill in life.

Key Takeaway

Try as many things as you can to figure out what you are good at.

4

Like for Raj, Comment for Dubai

*The people who are made fun of aren't stupid, it's
the people who make fun of them that are.*

High school, especially eleventh and twelfth standards,
is when you want girls to be interested in you and have
people look up to you. You want that social validation,
you want to be in that social circle that is fancy and rich.
So, I was like, 'Bro! I have to become cool.' I told my
classmates I went to Dubai in the summer vacations when
I hadn't even been to Delhi. I told them the beaches were
lit, the girls were hot, the buildings were so amazing.
I had an uncle who lived in Dubai, so I knew a lot about
it. I described Dubai to them with such conviction that
they believed me. I made it sound like it wasn't even a big
deal for me, that I visited Dubai whenever I felt like it.
And my social status in school skyrocketed.

Now that my classmates were interested in me, they
wanted to befriend my cousins. They went to one of my
cousins and asked her, 'Raj went to Dubai, didn't you

go?' My cousin looked at him and said, 'Do one thing, ask Raj if he has ever seen a passport in his life.'

So, from being the 'cool' guy, I became the school meme. Posts were put up on Facebook: 'Like for Raj, comment for Dubai.' I used to enter school and everybody would go, 'Oh! Look, look, look, it's Dubai.' I became famous as 'Dubai' in my entire school. Even my juniors would mock me with that name. You're in twelfth standard, you're the senior, and these kids in ninth standard, even they are making fun of you. Imagine the embarrassment.

As if that was not enough, the joke escalated and even the teachers started calling me Dubai. And if that was not enough, it went further and reached the coaching centres. And if even *that* wasn't enough, the joke reached my home. We are a joint family and when everyone was sitting at the dining table, my cousins would call me Dubai and everyone would have a good laugh. It was horrible. It was one of the saddest phases of my life.

There came a point when I didn't want to get out of my room. I was frustrated that I had become a joke. I locked myself in my room for a whole day and kept on crying. I wanted to end my life.

While I was sitting in my room, thinking about ending my life, I heard my mom shouting from outside, 'Raj, Raj, come here.' I went to where she was and I saw that my dad was shivering in bed and wasn't responding. As we rushed to the hospital, my dad said to me, 'Even if I'm not here, I know you will take care of your mom and brother.' And then, he lost consciousness.

Dad was taken into the emergency ward. After some time, a doctor's assistant came out and told us that he was unresponsive and that they were doing their best. I saw my entire life flash in front of me. Those few minutes still feel longer than the twenty-five years of my life.

Later on, we got to know that it was a diabetic attack and not a heart attack. My dad recovered and thankfully he's still with us. But that moment made me realize that I have to do something with my life.

Key Takeaway

The harshest realities of your life teach you the most important lessons.

5

Useless Kid with BIG Dreams

*Just because others don't question the choices
society has made for them doesn't mean you
shouldn't. Stop restricting yourself from doing
something that sounds crazy just because other
people your age are not doing it.*

I already had the Dubai incident to my name, I already was
a meme on Facebook, I already was a joke, I'd already had
the scariest moments of my life. I was done being the lazy
kid. I felt inferior and thought to myself that the only way
I could feel superior was by being richer than these guys or
at least be as rich as them. My thoughts at that time were:
I don't have to build myself up, I don't have to play sports, I
don't need to do anything. All I need to do is make money.

So, I did the most millennial thing ever. I went on
Google and typed:

'How to get rich?' *Enter*

A couple of articles popped up and I opened
multiple tabs but ended up reading only one. In that

it was mentioned, 'Start reading books if you want to become rich.'

I thought, 'Whoa! Great!'

Then I went on Google again.

'Top ten books to become rich' *Enter*

Again, I opened multiple tabs, and went through four or five of them. I noticed that one book was mentioned again and again.

Think and Grow Rich by Napoleon Hill.

So, I ordered that book. (And I still haven't finished it.)

I took the name of the book too seriously—I thought, I will think about getting rich and I will grow rich. I read a few pages of the book and I saw the book had been commissioned by someone called Andrew Carnegie, who was supposedly the richest man on the planet.

I thought, 'Let's put this book down and read about Andrew Carnegie instead.'

I went on Google again.

'How to become rich according to Andrew Carnegie' *Enter*

There was this one article that I read about him. I don't know which website it was, I don't even know how true to his ideas it was. But I felt like I needed to figure out a way to achieve my goal, and that's what led to my crazy plan.

Key Takeaways

1. Don't restrict yourself, keep exploring.
2. The lowest lows of your life pave the way for the highest highs if you are just ready to take that one positive step.

6

How to Become Rich

Guess what's the best thing about getting rich?
You only have to be right once. You can fail 999
times but if you get it right just once, boom! You
are going to the moon.

In the article it was mentioned that, according to Andrew Carnegie, if you want to become rich, you needed to do these three things.

First, have a business. You can't get rich by doing a job.

I don't know how true this is, really. In fact, I know people my age who are making 10x more money than me at their job. But, back then, I was convinced about this idea and that I had to have my own business to get rich. Ultimately, though, you have to choose what fits you, you don't need to have a business because I did it, you don't have to study a particular course because your best friend is doing it, and you certainly don't need to go for a government job because your parents did it. Not everyone wants to have a nine-to-five job; similarly, not everyone wants to be an entrepreneur or a content creator, and that is completely okay. Do what works for you.

I believe that people can be a really good number 4 or number 6, but they don't realize it. Everybody wants to become number 1. Not everyone can be a king. A few have to be kingmakers, and are very successful at that.

So I, a sixteen-year-old, wanted to start a business with zero experience. There were only two ways that I knew of. Come up with a product, service or an idea that doesn't exist, something crazily unique, like Paytm, Uber, Amazon. Or, come up with an idea that is already in the market, but with better value and better quality at a better price.

I didn't have enough brains to birth another Uber or Paytm. There's no way I could do this. So, I tried the other route. I decided to find a product that was already in the market, and come up with a better version of it.

Second, meet as many people as you can.

People are the best teachers. The more people you meet, the broader your mind gets. When you interact with people, your horizon is going to widen. You will expand your mind and push the envelope. The more people you meet, the more opportunities there are for you. The more you think, the better ideas you get. The better you can network and play the game in the world. And with all that, your chances of getting rich are higher.

So, I've made it a rule to reach out to one person a day, every day, for the rest of my life. I'm meeting one person a day, seven people a week, 365 people in a year, which is extremely powerful. How this rule helped me reach where I am is something I am going to tell you later on.

Third, start a business in the FMCG industry.

The last step of becoming rich, as per Andrew Carnegie, is to start a business in the FMCG industry. At that time, for me, FMCG meant a kirana store. In my town, the biggest of these were Big Bazaar and D-Mart. And I couldn't bring myself to go to Big Bazaar because I knew I couldn't buy anything, and I considered myself to be inferior. When you are from a middle-class family, you feel like Big Bazaar is some place only rich people can afford to shop at. It's when you are rich that you know you can go to a Big Bazaar, buy a biscuit and leave, or you can just roam around, buy nothing and leave. It comes with a level of confidence. Until and unless you are confident in yourself and know you have buying power, you don't feel comfortable to go to places that you think are fancy.

So, I started going to kirana stores nearby. One day, two days, ten days—I went and just observed people, seeing if I could find a product that could give me leverage.

I asked my father what I should do, and he said, 'Go and listen to the consumers, you'll get to know what they want and what they don't want.'

So, then, instead of just watching and listening to them, I started talking to the people who were buying stuff and to those who were selling them as well.

There were three things that I found out.

One, it is very easy to sell something if you can convince the women or the kids of the house. If you can manage to do this, your product is going to be in their homes at least for the first time.

Two, shopkeepers are the biggest influencers in India.

If they say something like 'Bhabhiji, take this product, *meri guarantee hai*', Bhabhiji can't say no. This is why I wanted to sell my product to the kirana stores; I knew shopkeepers could be my influencers. I just needed to convince them. I thought about how to come up with a product where the shopkeepers would get the maximum margin—this would convince them to sell my product.

Three, liquids became gold in 2013.

This was true across the FMCG industry. Body soaps were getting replaced by shower gels, hand soaps were getting replaced by liquid hand washes, and dishwashing bars were getting replaced by dishwashing gels.

While doing my 'market research', I found out that in the dishwashing gel category, there were basically two brands in India which were famous: Vim and Pril. At least, this was true in my city, and at that time my city was India for me.

So, I thought, 'Great! Only two products.' I thought, 'There are twenty lakh people here and only two brands. Boss! This is a lot of market to be captured.' That was my Eureka moment. I was going to hit the jackpot.

Then I went on Google again.

'How to make dishwash gel?' *Enter*

I found out how to make dishwashing gels on YouTube. I bought some chemicals and started experimenting at home in small glasses on a daily basis. I didn't have any facility for R&D, nobody was from a chemistry background in my family. My father knew a little about chemicals, and he guided me a lot. Nothing else. And I didn't have any knowledge or the money to get a consultant on board and get the formula.

I, along with father, tried eighty-six times and failed (it came to a point where my father got more obsessed than me with trying to get this product right).

The eighty-seventh time, with the help of my father, I figured out a formula with which we were able to make 500 ml of dishwashing gel for Rs 45. Vim and Pril were selling the same quantity with the same formula for Rs 110.

The market is moving towards liquid soaps and our product is a dishwashing gel—check.

Number two, the product is for housewives—check.

Number three, it has huge margins, so shopkeepers will be interested in it—check.

Great!

But the most important thing—the ground zero concept of my business idea—that my product needed to be better than existing products in the market and have a better price, was also met.

Bingo! That's it, Raj, there you go!

Key Takeaways

1. Do what suits you, be it a business or job.
2. You can be a really good number 4, you don't need to be number 1.
3. Come up with a business idea, choose your industry, meet as many people as you can.
4. It's okay to fail.

7

Begging: The Ultimate Student Power

When you feel like you have nothing, no experience, no connections, no money, you still have the biggest power of them all—the power to ask! Again and again till you get a yes.

I needed capital for my business, so I asked my father for money and he agreed. Now, I had my capital, I had my product, and it checked all my requirements. I thought, okay, my product is already for housewives, everything is going good. The question is, what can I do to make my product about kids as well? What could I do so both groups were involved?

Since kids are fond of sweet things, I decided to make the dishwashing gel smell like fruit. I added fruit pulp and the aroma of sweet lime. Kids would love it, and housewives would love it too. That was my selling point. So, I'd involved kids, I'd involved housewives, and I was giving maximum business margin. This was my business idea.

Only one thing was left: what if my formula burned somebody's hands or caused some kind of reaction? Because I didn't have any kind of chemical background, I didn't know whether my formula was safe or not. And I had only Rs 10,000 in my pocket, so I couldn't even afford a consultation with an expert.

So, I used my special student power.

The biggest student power is begging. Students beg everywhere for everything. They beg at home for permission to do things, they beg at college for attendance, they beg friends to lend them money, they beg restaurants for discounts—they just beg for everything. So, I used this power to convince people to help me out. I went on LinkedIn, because I knew that's where all the professional people were, and started begging there. I searched for consultants and people in FMCG. There was this one wise man who accepted my request. I reached out to him and messaged him some four–five times for a consultation. He was an ex-consultant for Henkel, Unilever and P&G.

He agreed to do it and said, 'I don't need your money, but I want you to realize that nothing in life comes for free. That's why I am going to charge 20 per cent of whatever your business' initial capital is, since a product consists of five things, and R&D is 1/5th of a product.'

He checked my formula, told me what I needed to do to make it better, and helped me to come up with a final formula that would be best suited for my product.

In return, he took Rs 2000 from my Rs 10,000. But now I was sure of my formula.

Now, with the remaining Rs 8000, I was able to make 200–250 500 ml bottles priced at Rs 45 each, and I had my stock ready to conquer the world.

From this initial stock, I gave out free samples to my college friends. The person using the product in their house liked it, and I got reorders. I expanded my reach and gave free samples to other students in my college, and later on to the entire college. And with every five free samples I gave, I received at least three reorders. I started selling in bulk, which was beneficial for both my customers and me. I came to be known as the dishwash king of my college and thus began my entrepreneurial journey.

Key Takeaways

1. You don't need millions in investments to back you in order to start something. Start with whatever you have, and grow it.
2. Keep trying different ways of reaching your goals, irrespective of how unconventional they are.

8

Be Ready to Look Stupid

*The only thing that is stopping you from growing
is your fear of looking stupid in front of people.*

One bad experience at school made me avoid public speaking altogether for years. I only started when I didn't have any option but to give a presentation in order to pass my internal examination in college. Even then I was scared that I would come off as stupid in front of everyone. Some people stop putting out their artwork because some random person on the internet made fun of them. Remember, people can only make fun of things you yourself are conscious about. Once you join them in the laughter and start taking the jokes, the laughter will stop.

We are always taught to seek validation from outside. When we are kids, our mothers tell us to go ask our fathers how we look. Right from that moment we start seeking external validation. That's the reason we take criticism from outside so much to heart.

Looking stupid is not just about your appearance; I am talking about the way you feel about yourself when you put your thoughts out there, bare and naked. Situations where you just wanted to be yourself and do your thing your own way. I'm talking about all the times you wanted to do what your heart wanted but you held back because of the fear of being judged.

All of us have felt that way at least one point of time in our lives. Even I did. But then I just stopped caring and started living a glorious life. How simple! Except it wasn't simple. It took a lot of effort and time. Before I started giving TEDx Talks and finally let myself come to terms with what I want to do with my life, I was scared to look dumb in public.

At first, I didn't want to look like an idiot in front of my family; later I was scared of making an utter fool of myself in front of a whole bunch of people who were going to hear me talk for the first time. But you know what? People are always going to have an opinion and I learnt that the hard way. You do something, they'll have an opinion. You don't do something, they'll have an opinion. Unsolicited, unwanted, never-asked-for opinions—way too many opinions.

But can we do something about this? Other than rolling our eyes 98,278 times? Yes! We can ask them to get out of our lives and live in peace. The only thing we need is to be self-aware. We need to be ready to look stupid.

I mean, how do you think people who invented great things like aeroplanes and mobile phones felt when they came up with these life-changing ideas? Those great personalities weren't sure what the outcome was going to be, but they were ready to risk their public image; they didn't care about the aftermath if their plans didn't work out. Their hard-earned respect was on the line, but they chose to do it still, even if it made them look like an idiot. That's exactly how great things are born—because of people brave enough to take risks.

I know that since childhood you've been conditioned to be conscious, to believe in yourself only when others do. You are allowed to feel that morale boost only after ten other people come and say great things to you. I've been in that place too. The saddest part is that no one has ever told me why we need this. Why do we need someone else to tell us about ourselves. Why are we giving someone else so much power over us? Screw what others have to say about you, VALIDATE YOUR OWN SELF because the fear of looking stupid is what holds you back.

This personal insecurity is screwing you in ways that you never dreamt of—it is pulling you away from being the next greatest personality. It's like that person who always rains on your parade. Don't give in to this. Just lift your middle finger to these insecurities and choose your own happy path. (Simple? Simple.)

'Just try new things. Don't be afraid. Step out of your comfort zones and soar, all right?' said the mighty Michelle Obama. So, listen to one of the most badass women of all time and soar, soar high in the sky. Decide your own limits and see the world open up for you.

Don't let the fear of looking stupid deprive you of all the heights that you could possibly touch. Accept yourself, because if you don't, then who else will?

And I know that everybody around you will say 'No! Take this slow' or even 'Who do you think you are?' These are the negative people around you.

Don't walk away from negative people, RUN.

You know exactly what you have to do. You just have to defeat your fear, stop caring about what others think and win at life.

Key Takeaways

1. Stop seeking external validation.
2. Keep trying new things.
3. Don't walk away from negative people, *run*.

9

Don't Focus on Your Goals

*You won't be able to achieve your goals if you
only focus on them; instead, focus on your daily
habits—that will dictate whether or not you will
achieve your goals.*

'Where do you see yourself in five years?' 'You have done
your graduation, what's next?' 'What is your ten-year
plan?' Be it a job interview, a prying relative or a concerned
friend, everyone keeps asking you, 'What next?', 'What
are your goals?' I say, to hell with your goals.

Why, you ask? Um, because I'm asking you to. Just
kidding! Basically, I'm asking you to not lose your sanity
over your goals because, trust me, that's exactly how
you'll royally screw up your own life.

I'll tell you how things went down with me when I
was trying to learn something as basic as driving a car. Of
course I was taught well by my instructor (my dad), who
advised me to not just take his car and hit the road, but
that I needed practice to perfect my driving skills.

Now, when we talk about driving, all we think about is pressing that accelerator or the brakes at the right time. But think again, is driving a car that easy? Do you really just need to focus on steering and those brakes while driving? No!

To drive a car, without practically landing in jail, you need to know more than just traffic rules, how to park, etc. Similarly, to achieve life's goals you need to do more than just identify what they are.

You need to have a path that'll take you to your destination.

You know, for the longest time in my life, even I just focused on what my goals were. I would obsess over scoring a good percentage in twelfth standard. I would literally wake up and go to sleep every day with that one thought stuck in my head. The young me thought that if I kept on feeding my brain with that idea, then maybe I would kick my own ass and do the needful. But the young me never sat down to map out how to get that good percentage. The naïve me never thought about what it is that I'm doing wrong. It took me all these years to finally figure out the importance of the process. I just never knew what the barrier between me and my grand success was. I just kept wondering what was pulling me down.

Now, finally, I know that the department I need to first take care of is my habits.

I need to keep track of what I'm doing, other things can go to hell. I need to be street smart and, at the same time, I need to plot my own success because—let's accept this fact—success won't be served to us on a silver platter, we'll have to earn it. I mean, I'm sure that, unlike Phoebe Buffay, we can have both—a pla and a plan.

Strive towards your goals, they say.

Strive towards your journey, I say.

Don't let your mind wander from your goals, they say.

Keep your mind off your goals, I say.

It doesn't matter how you reach your destination, what matters is that you've arrived, they say.

Your journey makes you the person you are, your destination is just the last stop, I say.

And this ideology works with every damn thing in life. Let's take another basic example, and I have a feeling that it is going to be very relatable to many of you.

Ever tried losing weight or gaining some? Well, I for one have tried losing it and, trust me, it didn't happen by just saying, 'My goal is to lose weight'. If it worked that way, then many of us would've literally said, 'I want to get six-pack abs' and lived happily ever after.

But do you know what worked for me and works for all those who have a fit (even chiselled) body? A fitness regime, a regime that makes them follow a certain diet and workout plan every bloody day.

They are the people who, instead of blindly obsessing over their goal, worked on their habits. Honestly, habits are something that we control, that we can train our brain to adjust to. Otherwise, usually, our pretty little human brain likes to overthink the overthinking and then we meet our old friend Demotivation, along with his 57,687 friends, Negative Thoughts.

What I am basically asking you to do is that yes, set goals, but focus far more on the process that'll get you there. Simply put in a system and follow it to reach your ultimate destination. You need to push yourself in the right direction, in the direction that takes you one step closer to your aim, one that doesn't mess with it. Also, beware of the fact that your goal is affected by factors beyond your control.

I realized what I really wanted to do in life without seeing that the hack to get what I wanted had been right there the whole time. All I needed to do was focus, focus on my daily routine, because that's where my secret ingredient to success is.

So, get your mind off that obsession and let this be the game-changer.

Key Takeaway

Instead of focusing solely on your goals, focus on finding ways to achieve them.

10

Just Stop Overthinking

*If you waste all your time thinking, when will you
get the time to live?*

Think before you speak, think before you wish for
something, think before you go, think before you take
any goddamn decision. Think, think, think. Aargh!
Thankfully, no one ever said 'think before you breathe',
or else, most of us would be dead by now.

By all means, think. But when you are constantly
thinking about one thing and worrying about it, it
becomes overthinking and that leads you nowhere in life
except backwards.

I'm sure most of you can recall your childhood when
your elders taught you to think before making a decision,
because decisions have consequences that you might not
be prepared for, ones that will affect your life in ways
that you cannot imagine.

But amidst so much thinking—overthinking,
actually—have you ever thought about what life would

be without all this contemplation? The only answer is that it would be much simpler.

Without overthinking, life gets ten times better. Honestly, thinking has caused me more harm than not thinking has ever done. It has burned more bridges than I was able to build in the first place.

This is how it works: imagine you have bought a new car and you have to drive eight hours from one city to another. But you keep focusing on things that could go wrong on the way, to a point where you think, what if there's a puncture, what if I am not able to find someone to fix that puncture, and then overthink a bit more, and before you know it, in your mind your car is on fire. But guys, it was an imaginary journey. If you ask me, overthinking messes with your brain in ways that you cannot even imagine.

I still remember when I was in high school. I wanted to get into my dad's business and take it to greater heights, but I made the mistake of overthinking. I found myself choosing computer science as a subject when I should've chosen entrepreneurship. And I chose computer science because I overthought all the other options I had. As a commerce student, I didn't want to take maths because I didn't want to go through the same torture of trigonometry in Class XI after my dreadful experience with it in Class X. I didn't want to take physical education because 'there's no scope', and how will this subject help me in the future? Then I started overthinking that if after school I am not able to do anything, I should have a backup, maybe build things through C++ and JAVA.

Yes! Computers seem to have a great future, so let me take computer science.

Now this decision was not because I was good at computers, or I knew something about them, but only because of overthinking that if everything goes wrong, I will still be able to do *something*. Because, according to society, if you don't take maths with commerce, you won't have any option in the future to do something good with your life, and that made me overthink and take a decision. Now I regret putting a little too much thought into one of the most important decisions of my life. (Important because, instead of going to two other tutors to learn something that I still didn't understand, I could have learnt something interesting or at least had fun with my friends as out of my class of sixty, only three people took computer science. Everyone else was having fun with other subjects.)

I'm sure most of you will relate to this because, as teenagers, each of us went through a phase where we just sat and thought about every damn thing. Why? Because we'd been told by everyone around us that every decision you make at this age will decide the kind of life you will lead in the future. Um, really? Think about it, is it really a logical approach towards living?

Imagine what would happen to your favourite athletes if they started thinking like crazies too. What happens when they lose and their fans are disappointed in them? Fandom can drive them crazy, you know? Nothing is worse than angry fans who just cannot accept that, like them, their favourite athlete can sometimes fail. If they sit and analyse the whole situation too much, then they are screwed for life. In fact, a lot of our favourite athletes actually suffer from depression at some point in their lives. Such is the power of overthinking. Which is why sometimes you need to not care and move on. Like Joey does. Yes, Joey from *Friends*. Yes, he would have fun; yes, he would not share his food—but care? I don't think so.

You need to shrug off all your worries and just do what needs to be done.

You know, worrying about the consequences of anything and everything is like crying over a breakup that hasn't even happened. And I don't think anyone needs that kind of negativity in our lives!

So, basically, my friends, you all need to just stop overthinking and worrying about the consequences of every action that you take because thinking is like a prison and your success is the prisoner. Once you set yourself free, once you stop giving things a second, third, fourth thought, you break free. You will stop thinking and start doing.

Do all that you can because you've got just one lifetime to prove your worth. This is your only chance to build the lifestyle that you've always wanted. Do it, live it.

Key Takeaways

1. Stop thinking, start doing.
2. There's something about your first gut feeling, listen to it—it might not always make the best decisions for

you, but it will always be the boldest one, and bold decisions without the thought of consequences can take you way ahead of other people.

11

Stop Innovating, Start Copying

None of us would've learnt anything if there was
nothing to copy from.

'Innovation distinguishes between a leader and a follower,' said the great Steve Jobs. Now, in our heads, a man who was a co-founder of a company like Apple, a company that doesn't need an introduction, must be a genius and we must believe everything that he says. Right?

Wrong! I don't think so. I mean, innovation is so out of trend now, please start copying because that is exactly where the fun lies. No, I am not encouraging you to plagiarize, I am simply asking you to get 'inspired' by other people's innovations and ideas. It doesn't really matter whether you're a leader or a follower if your deeds aren't of any use to you or to this world.

Take a moment and let that sink in.

Look at everything around you. Don't you see that whatever is being done or has been happening, in some way or the other, is inspired by something? Nothing is new, not even the idea of this book of wisdom that you're reading. Everything has been done before, everything gets built based on something that already exists in the universe. How else would we survive in the generation that has seen the best of this century?

For starters, let's talk about the nation's most successful start-ups. When we think of start-ups, we think of ideas—new and unconventional ideas. But do you think that the idea of Ola is original? It's inspired by Uber. What about Flipkart? Inspired by Amazon. Nothing is original, my friend. Not even the clothes that you are wearing right now, because the designer was also inspired by someone else's designs.

You see something new, you find out about the mind-blowing features of it and then you add your own touch to that something.

Basically, you copy, copy, copy and excel.

For a moment, let's keep the world aside and think about ourselves. Think about yourself. Who are you? Subconsciously, aren't you a person who is a mixture of influences and ideologies? You've also learnt and acquired these values and habits from a role model or a family member or a friend. Haven't you? People listen to me and tell me I remind them of GaryVee, the famous speaker and entrepreneur. That's because he is one of my biggest inspirations. I am a combination of every great person I admire—with my own touch.

You know, after speaking with an audience as huge as you all, I can safely say that if you ask an artist, a businessman or a founder of a company where they get their ideas from, the only honest answer would be, 'I steal them'. If you ask me where I get my speech ideas from, I'd happily inform you that I figure out what's worth stealing from this huge pool of content. I pick an idea, filter it and add some additional knowledge I have on that topic. I keep doing it and filtering it until I finally land on something that's worth sharing.

The bottom line is that everybody is doing that, guys. Every-goddamn-body.

'The only art I'll ever study is stuff that I can steal from,' said David Bowie. The man who tasted the best of this world clearly knows how to take his own share of success from this universe.

I don't know how many of you have heard about this ancient quote: 'Art is twice removed from reality'. Art is copied from reality and I cannot disagree with this one bit because, what do artists do? How do writers learn to write? How does a layman learn to play an instrument?

Don't we all just type a few words, YouTube it and there it is—the solution to all our problems? We all take pride in acquiring skills on our own, but each one of us knows that the only reason we were able to learn those things is because there were people who put up samples, videos, tutorials, mind maps, slide shows and audiobooks for us to learn from.

None of us would've learnt anything if there was nothing to copy from. Think about Facebook. I'm sure all of you must've watched *The Social Network* (if not, then what are you even doing with your life!), the movie that is based on Mark Zuckerberg, one of the most successful entrepreneurs on the face of the earth. What does our big guy do to make Facebook the kind of platform it is? He (apparently) used his seniors' ideas to build his own website. And look at him today, he is one of the youngest billionaires in the world and, I am sure, will never run out of business.

Do you know what the admired playwright Shakespeare did? No doubt the man penned down so many plays that went on to become classics. For many, literature is synonymous with Shakespeare, but you'd be surprised to know that even he believed in taking inspiration from other people's products.

Shakespeare wrote his tragic love story of Romeo and Juliet only after he learnt about Arthur Brooke's poem *The Tragicall Historye of Romeus and Juliet*. This 1562 poem was William Shakespeare's key source to the drama that today inspires many other filmmakers to create something that's one step ahead of Shakespeare's version.

Call it a vicious cycle or a loop, this is how the world works and this is how it has worked since eternity.

Start copying what you love. Copy, copy, copy, and at the end you're going to find yourself. I am not asking you to steal something from someone and make it your own, that's plagiarism. All I am saying is: be inspired and influenced by what is already around and make it your own.

Think of yourself as a devotee of some influencer, a devotee who keeps on taking all the great things from those multiple influencers that he follows on Instagram. Treat this world as an influencer and you be an influencee.

No matter how hard you try, you cannot copy someone perfectly. Have you ever tried signing on a paper multiple times? Were you able to make all those signatures look the same? No. A human hand isn't capable of making perfect copies. So, stop thinking about innovation. Try to copy your heroes, examine where you're lacking and then find out what's making a difference. Use that difference to transform and to create your own style.

Key Takeaway

Take inspiration from different places and create something of your own.

12

The 'vs' Game

*The easiest way to get rich is to become the
producer of the thing you consume the most.*

There was a point in my life when I used to go to
immersion sessions every three months. In these sessions,
the best people from each and every field come together
and share their knowledge with each other. But then I
realized I was taking knowledge from everywhere but
not spreading it. I was becoming a knowledge hoarder
instead of an executor.

That's the problem with our generation. We are in an
era of information overload. There is so much information
coming from everywhere and we keep consuming it. We
read books after books, watch videos after videos, buy
course after course and do nothing about it. We have
all become knowledge hoarders. We keep hoarding
knowledge and we expect to come out with better results
and make better decisions just because we have more
knowledge. And that's FALSE.

You need to be an executor so that you can find out where you are making mistakes, and then you can improve through that knowledge. Most people get into the process of learning and they just keep acquiring knowledge and they never manage to actually do anything in life. They are, maybe, one of the most knowledgeable people around, but they are not achievers. They aren't putting out their work. If you don't put out your work, if you haven't started writing, speaking or vocalizing your content in some way, then nobody would know that you are the best person to talk to about that topic. Now, I don't mean that everyone has to be a content creator and start a YouTube channel, but think about what you are doing every day. Whether you are working at a company as an employee, running your own business or just sitting at home chilling with Daddy's money, if you are not executing, talking about and acting on things that you learn from books, videos and courses on an everyday basis, what's the point? How will you improve and grow? In fact, if you are not going to take little steps and put in effort by applying your learning in real life, people won't even respect you, regardless of how knowledgeable you are.

'The easiest way to get rich is to become the producer of the thing you consume the most.'

Answer this one question today: Are you a consumer or are you a producer? This one question has the power to drastically shift your mindset from a person who is just thinking or dreaming about achieving big things to a person who actually achieves those dreams.

There are two kinds of people in life. Achievers, and those who think they want to become achievers, i.e., those who think, who admire people, but who don't do anything. I call them producers and consumers. We are all consumers. We all consume things. We go on Instagram, we keep scrolling, looking at people, we are consuming a lot of content.

We go on Google, we try to find something. We are consuming.

We play games all day, that's consuming.

But if you want to go somewhere with what you are passionate about, become a producer. Become a producer of the thing you are consuming the most by creating content about the topics you consume. Realize your interests through the things you consume and start taking that knowledge forward by spreading it.

Producers are the ones who produce, consumers are those who consume. The people who consume end up spending more, and people who produce end up earning more.

Producers win.

So many people come to me and say some variation of these things: I want to create content, should I leave my job and become a full-time content creator instead? My boss keeps on nagging me about something or the other, I want to be my own boss!

Are you someone who wants to leave your job and start creating content instead? Sure, you can. But let me tell you something, that is a lose-lose strategy.

You're giving up on financial security in order to chase an uncertain path that you don't know much about. What do you think is going to happen? You'll become an overnight success? 'Overnight successes' take ages to happen. When you see a content creator with a million followers, you see the glory and not the steps she has taken or the years it has taken her to reach that level.

Instead of dreaming of a superficial world and thinking content creators have the best life, try thinking in a logical way. I'm not saying you shouldn't become a content creator; all I'm saying is you don't need to leave your job in order to start the journey. Make it a side hustle till you have enough to make it your main hustle. Do it for a few months parallel to your job, see how it turns out, and once you think that the scale-up is feasible enough for you to do it full-time, then you can leave your job. But before that, it just wouldn't be practical.

Key Takeaways

1. Be an executor instead of a knowledge hoarder.
2. Be a producer instead of a consumer.
3. The people who consume end up spending more and people who produce end up earning more.

13

How to Be Successful

*If you learn how to have leverage over people,
success becomes easy for you.*

Anyone who is making money has some kind of advantage or leverage over other people. That is the reason they are making money. It may be because of the money they already have, or the way they speak, or their creativity; maybe their skills. One way or the other, they have some kind of advantage over other people. That is why they are higher on the ladder of creating wealth and branding.

Let's go back a few decades. Around the 1970s–1990s, when industrialization happened, the people who were making a lot of money were the ones who already had a lot of money. They had the leverage of wealth. We all have heard in our families, 'If you have money, you can do anything', haven't we?

Then came the 1990s–2000s. Those who were creating wealth were the ones who had the leverage of people. They were of the notion that I have a hundred people with me, which others don't, and I will form a union and my factory will produce the cheapest products. That is how China became wealthier.

Now, from the 2000s till around 2018, if you didn't have money, you needed people; if you didn't have people then you needed IP, that is, intellectual property, like coding or a very particular knowledge about something. For example, someone learns how to code and decides to build a useful app. Once the app is created, they sell it for a large amount of money. That is leveraging knowledge to create wealth.

Today, most people think, 'I don't have enough money to use as leverage. I am not inspiring hundreds of people to come and join me to have the leverage of people. I don't know how to code, or else I wouldn't be here reading this book.' So, what is the next big thing?

We have entered an era which works on specific knowledge and distribution. This is the era of media. The money is there, the people are there, the technology is there, so how do you get leverage? Through your specific knowledge. Some people are good speakers, that's why their videos are popular. Some people are good at acting, and that's what they are using to bring traction to their content. They are using their one specific knowledge or talent as leverage, and there's nothing more to it than that.

Let's take the example of video production. The only way you can make a lot of money through video production is when you have more knowledge and skills than the remaining 99 per cent of the people who are already in the market. You need to figure out that one thing that the 99 per cent don't know about but you do. That is the easiest way to make money in today's world.

Everything is already out there for you to be able to become better at what you do. If you learn about one thing for just six months—complete one course, read two books, read twenty blogs—you would be at least 10 per cent better than the rest of the people around you. All you need to do is follow one person who is already there, learn everything from them and when you think you have learnt everything, start following someone else.

Once you have acquired the knowledge, build a business around that, launch your own products, start consulting, or start your own course, and that is how you make money. Every skill is in demand in today's world— the only thing is how good you are at it.

You don't have to learn and become an expert at everything. All you need to do is become at least 1 per cent better than the 99 per cent of the people around you. That is how you start. It's that simple.

For example, you become a better communicator than ten of your friends, and you start telling them: 'Hey, you know what? I'll tell you how to write your essays, I'll tell you how to write social media content, I will even talk on your behalf on your Tinder account (it's going to be in high demand, trust me), you just give me Rs 1000 a month as a retainer.' Then you work on becoming better than 100 people out there, then 1000, then 10,000, then 10,00,000—keep climbing the ladder.

Now, some people will ask, how do I find the one thing to get better at? I'm not going to decide what that one thing is for you; someone else is not going to decide what that one thing is for you, it's YOU who is going to decide. Pick anything. Take the most basic thing—talking, for example—I picked that up. I used to talk a lot at school and I thought to myself, 'I talk so much, how can I monetize that? How can I learn more about this?' I then started learning more about it, and started talking more. After a period of doing that, I began making money by teaching others how to talk. After that, I took it to social media. All I do on social media is talk. There are approximately a million people following me now, and they want to hear me talk.

I will give you another example. There is a friend of mine who works at Dell. He earns Rs 2.5 lakh a month. That is an amazing job to have, right? When he was asked about his strength—that one thing that he could do better than everyone else—do you know what he answered? He said, 'I can stalk people on Instagram better than anyone else. I can go on someone's profile, stalk them for seven days, and tell you about their mother, father, what they do, the brand of food their sister's dog eats, the cities their friends belong to, how much they earn—I can tell you everything. I'm a gossipmonger and I love stalking people.' I'm sure most people love to do that, some do that with their exes, some with their crush, some with someone they're just interested in, but everyone is a good social media stalker. My friend's answer got him a job in the trend analysis department, where he has to look at influencers, see what they are doing and pick up patterns on social media so that Dell can come up with better campaigns and products.

If you are better than anyone else in one thing, you can land a job that pays Rs 2.5 lakh a month because the skill is not stalking—the skill is researching, keeping an eye on trends, finding out why everyone is doing some random dance steps on social media—that is the skill.

Directly or indirectly, consciously or subconsciously, we all have that one thing that we waste most of our time on. We think it's a waste of time but, technically, we are investing our time in getting better at that thing. The best way to identify it is to take a piece of paper, write down five things that you did today, things you felt you spent most of your time doing. It can be sleeping, talking, attending courses—anything. Even if it's your work that you think you wasted your time at, write that down as well—write down, I wasted my time talking to my colleagues, or whatever it is. Now, add a plus next to everything you enjoyed doing and a minus next to those things that you didn't enjoy. Do this for one week and by the end of it, pick up all the things you marked with a plus and figure out what is at the core of it.

Let's say you confessed to being an overthinker and wasted your time overthinking. '*Ye kya koi skill hai*? Can I monetize it?' Yes! You can become a very good strategic thinker. A strategic thinker is only paid to think, they are not paid to execute. If you are an overthinker, you already have a strategy because you are constantly thinking— what if this happened? What if that didn't happen? All you need to do is tell this to a business person. 'You know what? If you take this decision your business can really suffer.' Your job is to think. So even if you're wasting your time overthinking, you can monetize it.

What do you have to do? First, identify that you overthink a lot. Second, figure out a course that is related to thinking. Third, find a person who is already a strategic thinker. Don't believe me? No problem. Have you heard of Deloitte? Ernst & Young? PriceWaterCoopers? KPMG? You've heard of these companies, right? These are some of the biggest companies in the world, and they get paid to think. What are consultants and strategic coaches? Those who overthink a lot for you. You literally pay people to overthink for you. That's a goddamn skill.

So, you did that plus/minus thing for seven days, realized where you spent most of your time, and once you get to know that this is the place I'm spending most of my time, you realize that it comes naturally to you.

Nobody does something for a whole week if it irritates them. If you are doing something continuously, it means you are enjoying it and it comes naturally to you. You are doing it not because you're wasting time, you're doing it because you have a tendency to do that thing. All you need to do is to shift your perspective. Keep doing this for a month and, by the end of it, you'll find out your niche—the one thing that you really love doing.

Once you have figured that out, find the right person in that field, follow them, and do what they are doing. If they're selling a course, buy it; if they're doing a live event, watch it; whatever that person is doing, do that for the next thirty days and you will find out how they are able to sell a skill you also possess. That is the fastest way to make money in today's world.

Find out the one thing that is very easy for you to do and that is difficult for other people. Ask yourself, how can I monetize this? And then think of a way to do it better than a hundred people, a thousand people, a million people. The more people you can do it better than, the better the leverage you have and the more chances of you being successful or making money.

Tell me one thing you think you can't make money at, and I will prove you wrong.

Key Takeaways

1. Learn and become at least 1 per cent better than the 99 per cent of people around you.
2. You have to decide what is the one thing you are good at; no one else can decide it for you.
3. Figure out how to monetize the thing you are good at.

14

How to Come Up with a Business Idea

You can build a business in every field, it's all about how good you are in that field.

When it comes to becoming an entrepreneur, you need to figure out if you have a good idea. If you have a good idea, there's no right or wrong time to start. But if you're coming to me and saying, 'Bro! I want to become an entrepreneur, I want to start my own business, but I don't know where to start', then here is how I got my first business idea.

I'll decode the three simple ways I went about getting my first business idea. They still help me come up with new business ideas even today. These steps are for both people who don't have a business, and those who do have a business but want to venture into new areas.

Step 1:

Choose your industry

Choose the industry that you are passionate about, because it's a lie that some industries have big money and some don't. Each and every industry in the goddamn world has some money. Trust me on this. I have looked up so many cases and I'm still trying to find an industry that doesn't have money and/or successful people in it.

So, no matter which industry you choose, you can be successful in it—but you have to choose only one industry. Choose the industry you are obsessed with, about which you read the most, and watch videos of. Do you find yourself watching fashion reels all day? Or do you read about every car's top speed, features, launch date? What do you spend the maximum time on—Bollywood gossip, business news, creator economy? What? Analyse that.

In my case, I chose FMCG because I loved reading about every product, their manufacturer, their marketing ads. I loved learning about how Amul became Amul, how Brooke Bond Tea became famous, or why Bisleri is the only bottled water brand we know of. That's why I chose FMCG. In your case, it might be automobiles or automation or technology, or you might want to get into mobiles or software or metals or infrastructure or sports or entertainment. WHATEVER. Choose one industry. You need to be crystal clear and you need to be very focused on this part. It all starts with that one thing, with that one industry.

It could be a mix of reasons why you choose an industry. With me, maybe I was interested in FMCG because my father was already in that industry and he is my hero. And then, I also wanted to get into it because I thought that serving many people at large on a lesser margin was going to be a better strategy for me, since I love selling. I worked on this model called high volume, low margin. Maybe for you it will be different. You might want to go into real estate, where it will be low volume and high margin.

Once you have chosen your industry, then comes the second step.

Step 2:

Find out where your strength lies
What are you good at? Is it writing, speaking, observing, building, selling, coding, designing? What do you think you do best? And by best, I mean out of ten things that you can do, what is that one thing you can do better than all the others? Like I know how to play the guitar, write a rap song, find good stocks by reading about a company and a hundred other things, but I feel the thing I can do best is tell a good story and inspire people to take action.

So, find out what your strength is. You don't know what it is? Prepare dinner at home and invite five–ten people you are close to. People who know you well: best friends, parents, cousins, neighbours, whoever. Then ask them: Tell me honestly, what do I suck at? Like what do you think I can't do at all so I should not even try to build a career in that. After they have humiliated you enough and you can't take anymore, stop them and ask them, now tell me what do you think I do best? Is it that I prepare good presentations or cook well, or talk well, or just listen well? Whatever they tell you, the thing which gets most votes, try pursuing that for a while. If you also feel that it's your strength, congratulations! If not, keep doing that again and again after every six months till you find it.

Step 3:

Find a problem where your strength can be used best
Now that you've zeroed in on your industry, try to find out the problems in this industry which can be solved through your strengths. In my case, a new category—liquids—was developing, but it was expensive. So, I made a cheaper alternative and used my storytelling strength to come up with a new story about fruit pulp in dishwashing gels, which soon enough the entire city started talking about. It was not a revolutionary product, but the story was new for the city, which helped me grow.

Bonus Step 1:

Choose your product
As I mentioned earlier, there are two ways to get into business. You either come up with an idea that doesn't exist in the market, like Uber, Paytm, Zomato or Amazon, or you come up with the cheaper, better version of a

product that is already there in the market. I chose to go the second way. I came up with a cheaper alternative of an existing product but offered better quality. One way of going about this is, you can get a job in the industry that you are interested in. Once you are there, try to figure out how the entire system works, try to find out the problems in that particular industry. And once you figure out what these particular issues are, you can build your business trying to eliminate those problems in the product.

After you have picked your product, the last thing would be:

Bonus Step 2:

Observe

No matter who your buyers are, no matter where your market is, just start spending time with them, go to that market and observe. In my case, back in 2013, when I started my FMCG business, the best place I could find to do market research and observe was a really small grocery store near my house. I went and stood there for two–three hours. Then I went to another one, and another one, and another one. I would observe sales patterns and the customers. That's how I found out that the entire market was shifting to liquids: shower gels, liquid hand wash, liquid detergent. I couldn't have found this out any other way.

Coming up with a business idea is the easiest thing; all you need to do is follow these steps and be observant. After doing these three things, all you need to do is launch your product. And then, trial and error and customer feedback are going to help you out. I kept on making errors, I kept on getting customer feedback and I kept on improving, and that is how I built a business empire from Rs 10,000. And you can do the same.

So, that was when you didn't know what you wanted to do. Once you have an idea that you want to work on, try to figure out who your target audience is. How to sell is never a problem if you know who you are selling to. If you know who to sell the product to and the person who needs your product, then the sale will automatically happen.

A while back, my team and I were brainstorming on how to scale up my digital marketing business and how to get a few clients in order to make it sustainable. We realized that how to sell is not even a problem. All we need to do is find people who want to build their personal brand, who don't have the time to focus on it, but have the money to afford the kind of services we are offering. Find the audience. That's it!

Key Takeaways

1. Zero in on the industry you love.
2. Find out what your strengths are.
3. Start observing.
4. Launch your product.
5. If you know whom to sell to, how to sell won't be a problem.

15

How to Price Your Product

India is price-sensitive first, so if you are building something here, make sure you get this right, because bad price and good product leads to failed businesses in this country.

No matter which category you belong to, there's this one common question: How to decide a price for your product or services. You might be an entrepreneur venturing into the business world for the first time in your life, wondering how much you should charge for your product. You might be someone entering the freelance world, confused how to decide the charges for your services. Or, you might be someone starting a new job, trying to figure out your salary.

Let's say you are a writer. You decide to charge Rs 100 to write a book of 50,000 words, and twenty people are interested in hiring you. When there are twenty people, you know you can increase the price. Now you decide you can charge Rs 1000 for a book. If there are twenty people ready to pay you for your work, you realize you can charge Rs 10,000. If there are ten people ready to pay you, you know you can charge Rs 10,00,000. Then you'll be like okay, I have only one client now. Great! Even if only one client comes, it doesn't matter, I can do it and it will still be worth it. You increase your price based on how many people are ready to pay you for your product.

How do you calculate the price of your service? You calculate it on the basis of your time. If you have eight hours in a day and you're making Rs 1,00,000 a month and the other person cannot offer you that, then to hell with him. But if you're working for Rs 50,000 and someone is ready to pay you Rs 1,00,000, then you would be more than willing to do that. Bingo! You have increased the price of your product and services. You just decide a price and try to increase it bit by bit. You try to price your time.

First of all, everybody needs to have an hourly rate. Make sure you communicate to your client that you are ready to give x hours for the work; if it takes more than that, then you are going to charge for every extra hour. Make sure the other person understands that there's a code of conduct that needs to be followed.

You should compare your hourly rate with how much you would be getting if you were doing a regular job. Suppose you could get a job for Rs 30,000 a month and you're working ten hours a day, then your hourly rate becomes Rs 100. Now if you have to provide a service to someone, make sure you're charging at least Rs 110 per hour. Because if you are spending your hours on stuff that's not work, then you need to make more than you do while working in your office.

If you have no job and you're earning zero rupees, then just start doing it for free so that you build a name for yourself. The faster you make a name for yourself, the faster you can start charging money, and then keep increasing your fee.

What do you do on social media? You tell them this is a trailer; if you want more, then pay for it.

Suppose you come to me and tell me, 'Raj, I want you to write me a speech. How much do you charge?' I will tell you, 'You know what? The average person with these many years of experience charges x amount, the person who has given fifty speeches and has 100k followers on social media charges x amount. What do you think, given my time and my calibre, I should charge? I have given you the power. How much do you think I am worth?'

You might try to joke around and say, 'If it's up to me, I want you to do it for free, yaar, take Rs 50.' And my reply will be, 'Okay bro, you know people who would do it for Rs 50, go and get them to do it. If you came to me then you must think there is some merit.'

The same power shift rule applies here. You have given the power to someone else to decide. If you agree with the amount they come up with, then cool, go ahead with the work. If you don't and think there's scope for negotiation, negotiate. But if you think this person is not valuing your time and effort and you'd get more with your job or through other projects, then simply tell them, 'Thanks for the offer, I see you don't have the budget right now. I look forward to working with you when you do have the right budget.' That's it. If the person recognizes your value, they'll try to retain you. If they can't, move on.

Key Takeaways

1. Decide the price of your product or service depending on how many people are willing to pay you for it.
2. Put a price on your time.

16

The Number One Rule
of Selling

*You sell better when you focus more on 'what am I
giving' and less on 'what am I gaining'.*

Selling is basically the use of information available
in order to get what you want. There are three kinds
of information availability: information disparity,
information parity and information overload. Sellers
adapt to each to sell their products.

Information disparity
This is when the salesperson knows more about the
product than the buyer. Let's say, when our parents or
grandparents went to buy a car, the salesperson in the
showroom knew much more about the car than them. So,
they could effortlessly convince or manipulate the buyer
and easily sell the car. The ball was in their court.

Information parity

Then came the era of information parity, where everybody had access to information on everything. The buyers were as knowledgeable as the seller. If they wanted to buy a hatchback, they could research what each brand offered, and at what price point. The seller couldn't fool them.

Information overload

Now, we live in an era of information overload. In this era, the buyer knows much more than the seller because of the internet. Everything is just one Google search away. You want to know what other people thought of a product, just go on Amazon; want the best price—that's available too. It's hard to fool buyers now. That's what information overload means.

You cannot sell to somebody who already knows everything about a product. They will only buy if they trust you. The market is full of people selling the same thing, so who you trust is what matters. Now, the person you trust is the person you buy from. And that is why personal branding is very important. From the selling era, you have to move to the personal branding era if you want to go up a level or accelerate sales.

You have to make people trust you and your brand.

How do you build that trust?

By generating awareness, keeping your promises and over-delivering, every time.

It's simple logic. It's caring.

The number one rule for marketing is caring.

Once you start caring about other people, then everybody in the entire value chain is going to trust you. And once people start trusting you, you can command the kind of premium you were looking forward to.

Key Takeaways

1. If you know how to use the information platforms available to you, you can sell anything.
2. Care about what you are selling and to whom you are selling.
3. Use personal branding to start selling.

17

How to Sell a Product

Prepare the product, package it with emotion and make it feel like it's urgent—that's it; that's how you can sell anything. I call it the P+E+U method (preparation, emotion, urgency).

Why would somebody buy from you? If you want to sell, you need to understand your buyer. People buy things because they need them. Why would they want to buy from you? Because you have something they need.

The first part of selling is preparation. Why did you buy this book? Because you thought I knew something that you need right now. In the same way, you need to have a specific product or knowledge in a specific domain that the other person doesn't have.

Once you have knowledge about something—for example, I know how to create wealth, and I know how to build a personal brand and capitalize on it. I know the formula to it; *Raj Shamani ne figure out kar liya hai.*

I have a specific knowledge and I know that people need what I know.

Now, we come to the million-dollar question. Why will somebody buy from you? They will only buy because of either of two emotions: fear or aspiration.

Nobody will ever do anything in their lives if there is no fear or aspiration. Every decision we make, every product that we buy, either improves our lifestyle or makes us feel secure. Why would you get out of your bed and start working? Because you're scared you'll be kicked out of your house if you can't pay rent. Most people probably have a drive to work because of their fear of the future, of going hungry or being unable to provide for their family. Or it could be aspirational—you don't like your current reality and you want to change it and go one level up. You aspire to be something you are not today.

So, how do you target one of these two emotions as a seller? First, you need to become better than the average person, or else the average person won't buy what you're selling. Second, you need to figure out what emotion is driving the person you are selling to. Either you create an aspirational scenario, like, you know what, if you buy my book today then your life can also get better, like mine has. You read the book and follow the principles in the book and you will be at the same place that I am. That could be one way of selling. Or, it can be forceful. You buy my book or else, considering the fast pace that the world is moving at, you will be left behind and won't be able to get anywhere in life. Universities are not teaching you what you need to know. So, there's a fear of not having a job tomorrow if you don't learn something today.

Now comes the third part. Objection handling. Suppose I tell you that you need this book because, if you don't read it right away, you're not going to be able to get ahead and win. So, I told you this and you understand the need for it as well, but you want to buy it tomorrow, not today. Procrastination. Humans are procrastinators. Our brain tells us, 'Bhai! Take it easy today. We'll see what happens tomorrow.' You think, 'If I buy the book, I will have to read it at night. Why should I read the book tonight when I can watch *Friends* on Netflix instead?' This is where the third part of selling, that is, objection handling, comes in. You have to create a sense of urgency. 'Bro! You need to buy this book today! Otherwise, the moment we see a recession, your job will be gone and then no one will hire you. You need to equip yourself with knowledge that can help you stand out. All those people who read this book will know how to sell, but you won't. So, buy and read this book today!'

Let's take the example of crypto. The crypto companies are not saying you should use their wallets because they're the best. They're saying you should use their wallet to buy today because tomorrow it will go up. You become part of that 1 per cent of people today who will not regret tomorrow. The rest will regret tomorrow that they did not buy it today. Do you want to be part of that 1 per cent or the 99 per cent? That is what crypto companies are trying to advertise, FOMO.

Let's take another example. Suppose you call a client to sell a SaaS product. Let's see how a conversation with objection handling will go.

You say, 'Sir, we had a meeting, you know the details of the product, you liked it, then what is the reason you are not buying it?'

The other person says, 'Yaar, I'll take a look next week; I don't have time right now.'

(Then you handle the objection.)

'Sir, exactly! I know you don't have time, that's why I want you to finish it right here, right now. Because even I don't have time. We both have better things to do with our lives. Why extend it to next week when we can finalize it in two minutes. You tell me and we will get it done. Is there any other issue I can resolve?'

(You handled the objection of time. You said, I understand, and that's why I'm calling you today, because I know you're going to be busy tomorrow. Every day your company is growing, and your time is becoming more and more valuable. That's why I don't want to waste your time tomorrow on something that you can do today.)

'Yaar, my company is in deep losses. I don't have the money right now to buy your product. That is the actual reason. I was just giving you excuses. Next month, when money comes in, I'll buy it.'

'Sir, I know. I know that your company is not making enough money because you are losing it on other SaaS products which are not working efficiently for you. I want you to save money from day one—from today itself. I know it's a leap of faith, that's how all of it happens. You have faith that tomorrow things will be better, I am telling you there is a way to do it today. I want you to save money. That's why I am telling you that my product is the most cost-efficient product right now. It will help you in tracking, it will help you earn more money in the long term.'

(You handled another objection.)

Now the person starts opening up to you.

'Yaar, my boss won't agree. If someone else tells him about it, he'll agree, but if I tell him, he won't. You should try the other person.'

'That is the reason I am reaching out to you. Because I know this is way more important for your credibility than mine. If you, rather than any other colleague, go to your boss with a product that helps him out, your reputation is going to go up and you will be remembered at promotion time because you saved them millions of rupees this quarter.'

Sold!

This is what objection handling is. You handle all the objections and create an urgency till the other person is convinced and decides to buy the product. That is how you sell.

Preparation, driving emotion and objection handling.

Key Takeaway

Find the driving emotion and learn how to tackle objections that come your way, and you'll sell anything.

18

How to Negotiate

*If you want someone's money, show them how
you can make their money work for them.*

How do you negotiate with someone? Negotiation is
a game with just one rule—managing the power shift.
What does it mean and how does it work, you ask?
Simple. Make the other person feel like they're winning.
And when do people feel like they're winning? When they
feel powerful.

Negotiation is nothing but a psychological ego game.
While negotiating, people want to feel that they are smarter
than you. So, all you have to do is stroke the other person's
ego. Make them feel they've got the better of you. How do
you do that? By shifting the power dynamic. This means
that you make the other person feel more powerful than
you. You do it by first talking about the deal, then shifting
the conversation to hype up the other person.

Ask them questions. What do you think my worth
is? What kind of premium should I command? Should I

charge 10x other people because I have 10x the followers? You start putting things in perspective. You make them feel valued. Once you start doing that, you can sell them a tree.

For me, it's not about money, it's about time. If I take out time for someone else, I make sure the reward is higher than what I'd get if I spent it on what I love doing.

One thing to always keep in mind is to never state your price first—let the other person quote something.

Why is that, you ask? Because if you are the one to state a price first, then you have to stick to it. Then you will have to negotiate on the basis of the perks, and not the price.

Let's say I charge Rs 1 lakh to work on a speech. Some people would say, bro, that's too much. I'll tell them to find someone else. But I know that I have ten people ready to pay me Rs 90,000 for a speech, that's why I have increased it to Rs 1 lakh. Let's say the other person says that I really want to work with you but I don't have that budget. So you say, okay, instead of three revisions I will do four revisions for you. Instead of giving you two hours of my time, I'll give you two hours twenty minutes of my time and in those twenty minutes, I'll help you prepare to deliver that speech as well. You keep on adding benefits, but you do not reduce the price.

Focus on how you're making that person feel: if they feel like you're doing something extra for them, like the power is in their hands, they'll think, this guy's bringing so much value, let's give him what he's asked for. He's the best, that's why he is charging this much. Tell them,

I'm charging x amount not just because I'm the best and have done so many things, but because my time is limited. Give the other person the power to decide whether or not to hire you, but never make them feel like you're open to negotiating your fee. You have to make the other person feel like that would be an absolute no from your side.

You tell them, if they think someone else can do it, then great, let them do it. It's called comparison analysis. You compare yourself with the other people in the market. Apart from disclosing your price first, you tell them everything else. If you do a price comparison, then people will always consider the one who is cheaper. Then there is no value in you, right? You have to make them see the value you are generating instead of the price you are charging.

Back in 2014, I wanted to advise Jaguar Land Rover on their social media campaign on Facebook and Google. When I went to their office as a college student, I told them, 'I love this car, and that's why I want you to be on top of your game when you launch it. That's why I want you to be the first in central India to get on the digital platform.' Back then, nobody was actually doing much on digital media.

Jaguar asked me why I was telling them all this. I said I wasn't doing it to sign them on as my clients. I was giving them advice because I had a dream that, one day, I would have this car. That's what made me tell them to do something no other car company was doing back then—because I wanted to help them.

They asked me what exactly I was offering them. I said, I can tell you who *exactly* are the high net-worth individuals living in a specific upmarket neighbourhood. I can directly tag these people and show them ads, get their responses and their numbers and email ids and give you the details in the next seven days.

I told Jaguar that for the reach this marketing will have, you would have to get a billboard in a posh locality for Rs 5 lakh a month. Even then, there's no guarantee that your target audience would notice the ad. Or you would have to post an ad in a newspaper, which would be Rs 2 lakh per day. So, what do you think? If I can give you that data in seven days instead of a month, how much would that be worth to you? Because even if you spend Rs 5 lakh in a week, that would be better for you because you'd save three weeks, during which time you could take other important decisions.

So, you tell me how much that is worth to you. I'm not doing this because I want Rs 2000 from you. I'm doing this because I genuinely love this car and one day dream of having this car, and I would like it if I'm able to make this brand a leader in the market. That is why I am doing it.

With this, I've shifted the power to their hands. I've told them two things: you decide the price, and that I'm not doing this because I want their money, I'm doing this because I genuinely love this car.

They came up with a price and said we think we can take this on a trial basis and give you Rs 1 lakh for it. At that time, I needed Rs 23,000.

Most people lose at negotiation because they come directly to the price. They straightaway say I'll give you a 15 per cent discount. Why on earth would you give a discount? There should be a reason. Give them the reason. First off, if you can't decide your price, that means you've done your homework wrong, you don't know your price, you don't know what your worth is. If you're not earning anything and you are getting Rs 100, it is favourable for you, right? The problem with people is they have no money, they have no clients, but think clients who will pay Rs 50,000 are cheap. They only want those who can pay Rs 1 lakh. Bro! You don't even have 500 bucks, at least you're getting Rs 50,000, take it.

One more thing to keep in mind is that you never negotiate in a hurry. Negotiation is always done with time, selling is done quickly. If you don't have time, that means you are selling, and if you don't get time, that means you are a bad salesman.

Key Takeaways

1. First rule of negotiation—power shift.
2. Second rule of negotiation—power shift.

19

The Three Kinds of Observers

The biggest superpower you have is the ability to observe; the more observant you are, the better your chances of winning in life.

A lot of people ask me what is the one skill they need to learn to get ahead in life. What should they do to get better in their business or job, or just how to get better in life in general?

Understand human behaviour.

That is the three-word answer. You just need to understand how humans behave.

I'm dead serious about this. You need to learn why people talk a certain way; why people buy what they buy; what is the decision they are making in the moment they're buying something? Why do they like some videos and not others? Why do they leave good reviews, or why are they not giving good reviews?

You need to understand all of this. It's the one skill that is going to take you far ahead in life.

Now, the question is, how do I learn human behaviour?

It's very easy. By observing.

Or you can read books on psychology, talk to psychologists, go through the profile of your competitor and read all the comments and reviews.

It'll help you understand what people want, what they appreciate and what they dislike.

And once you begin to understand all of this, you are going to make better decisions in life.

Everybody who is at the peak of their career is an observer. Everyone who is an observer and backs up their observation with the right execution becomes an achiever. The point is, how do they decide where to focus their observation skills? By not letting someone else dictate their curiosity.

There are three kinds of observers. Number one: those who have always been forced to do something. Since the beginning, they have their target set for them— Mummy said it has to be IIT and only IIT. Even if they are interested in playing the guitar, they won't be able to. They've been conditioned so much by their family that they start to believe that getting into IIT is their only possible option. They've always been dictated to.

They do reach the top because they have been told since the beginning the specific things that they have to do and not do. But they lack one thing, and that is mental peace, because they are always under constant pressure. They are excellent achievers, they'll come first in class, they'll crack IIT, lead companies, become CEOs, they'll achieve everything, but they will always be physically and mentally exhausted.

Their entire life someone else has set their finish line, which they must reach at any cost. The only way they know how to survive in life is to cross that line, one dictated by someone else. They don't think about anything, all they know is to do what they are told by their parents or mentors. Let's call this the Asian Parent Syndrome.

When you are not thinking about anything, you observe patterns based on the realities that are forced on you. So, if your parents tell you that students going to IIT and Harvard have the best life, you go to Google, you search Harvard alumni or IIT alumni, you look at their lives and you are like, 'Wow! People who go to Harvard are like Barack Obama.' They think the pattern is that people who went to Harvard have become presidents. It is set in their minds that if they want to achieve something in life, Harvard is their only option, or that their career is over without IIT. They observe the pattern and make that forced reality their own reality. They start working for it, but they are always exhausted.

The second kind of people are those whose achievements are driven by emotions. Feelings of inferiority or rage are what drives them. If you look closely, most people who achieve big things in their lives have an inferiority complex. They feel they don't belong where they want to belong. They think, 'This is my reality, I am not rich, I want to change this inferiority complex into something else,' and they start working towards it.

That was an extreme example, let's take a very basic example. Let's say you have four classmates, but why does this guy get to talk to the one girl I like? And then you start hating that one person and you want to be better than him, because he gets the limelight everywhere.

You will find these people in offices as well. There's this one guy who always gets the promotion, who always gets a better appraisal than everyone else, who is always the boss's favourite. You think to yourself, 'I do all the work, then why is he getting a promotion?' Then you start to do everything you can just to prove that you are better than this guy. You eventually do become better and get the things you wanted—except the girl, maybe. (Remember Suniel Shetty's character in *Dhadkan*?)

It can be as simple as some people deciding to show their parents what they can achieve, like Ranbir Kapoor in *Wake Up Sid*. Some people might want to get rich to win their parents' hearts, like Ranbir Kapoor in *Bombay Velvet*. Or the famous formula—heartbreak makes you a better singer, like Ranbir Kapoor in *Rockstar*. Basically, all Ranbir Kapoor movies are based on the second category of people.

The people in this category generally land up in creative fields. They start observing the patterns and think, Oh! a life of hardship can bring success. They think that this is something that happens a lot, and as a creative person they're always trying to find this negative emotion in their lives. They think: Just wait and see how I rise after suffering this terrible thing.

While those in the previous category of people had someone else's reality forced on them, in this category, you wilfully start adapting to the common narrative. You are influenced by your emotions, or you are influenced by someone's story, which raises a kind of emotion, and then you start observing the patterns in your own life to become someone like them. Eventually, because of these things, you start working on yourself and achieve what you want in your life.

Even though you become an observer, your observation is driven by your emotions, or from someone else's reality, which you feel, because of certain situations, is your own reality as well. You start finding patterns to belong to the narrative.

The people who belong to the second category feel empty. It's because they are always chasing something that is not their own reality. They end up wondering why they worked so hard for their achievements. They often ask: What now? I've become a singer, now what? They are also good observers but have a constant feeling of emptiness.

Then there's the third kind of people, those I call the rational optimist. These people are optimistic about everything in their lives. They have a very strong sense of self-belief. Because their parents never told them that they must do a particular thing, they are naturally curious and open to exploration. Their parents gave them the liberty to do what they wanted. They aren't driven by false emotions and are emotionally strong people. They are very rational and logical. Going to IIT doesn't matter to them. They believe if they learn something they are interested in, if they invest time in that and keep doing that thing again and again and again, they'll become the number one person in that category. They think, even if I'm an expert on bottles, I'll be the best at it. So, one day Bisleri will come to me with an offer. 'Bro! You are the expert in bottles in the country, come and join us. We will give you Rs 5 lakh a month.'

These kinds of curious people generally end up with jobs that require them to be innovative or entrepreneurial or scientific. They get obsessed about one thing and they observe only that one thing because they feel the outside environment or emotions is not enough to inspire or influence them. Their inner desires dictate their lives. They observe something that they are drawn to, they come to a conclusion which dictates their lives, and they achieve something.

They do not get distracted by whatever is the next new thing in the world, or look around for someone whose heart has been broken and follow that story, or say, 'My mummy and papa told me to study at this university only.' They get obsessed with one thing and do it, like Steve Jobs.

The drawback that this category of people have is the obsession. Such people stop looking at the world around them. They don't have healthy relationships and they don't have friends. They are obsessed with this one goal, and they are fired up by the idea of changing the world with it, because they know they have that potential in them. They feel everything they are learning is taking them one step closer to their one big vision.

The most successful of these entrepreneurs are rational optimists. They are optimistic that one day they will shake up the world, but they are also rational in their approach. They won't leap off a building expecting to turn into Shaktimaan. They'll be like, humans can fly, so they'll make some gravity-defying thing and then they will fly.

I feel like, earlier, I belonged to the second category, but now I'm shifting towards the third category. I'd like to believe that being successful is moving from the second category towards the third category. Most people start their journey with an inferiority complex, because if you feel you are the best in the world, why would you ever want to get out of your bed and start working on yourself? If you feel you are not enough, that your lifestyle is not enough, that forces you to do certain things. The only thing is your life shouldn't become a constant chase. Shift from the second category to the third category. When you reach the third category and you know you are a rational optimist, you understand the factors in the market. When you understand that every action you take has an equal reaction out there, and you can change the course of your own reality, it doesn't matter whether some people understand your status or not, whether your parents force their reality on you or not, all of these things stop mattering. You can change the course of your own reality without having any emotion, without having any guidelines from your parents or your elders or anyone else. That is a very sweet spot to be at.

All three categories of people are good observers. That's why they are successful and have reached their goals. Everybody is an observer; what you focus on, what you do with your observation is what defines where you are going to reach in your life. I would say: be a curious observer. As I said earlier, no question is stupid. You just need to be curious about stuff, and you'll find out which questions you're most interested in. You start finding answers for your questions. You will find a pattern, you will connect those patterns one day, and that will help you with your own innovation. And if not innovation, it will help you become self-aware, and then you'll know what to do with your life and how to live it.

Key Takeaway

To move ahead in life, you need to understand human behaviour—what people do and why they do it.

20

How I Decide My Content

You don't need to be intelligent; you just need to
be average, again and again.

I believe there are two parts to creating good, relatable content. One is the kind of person you are, and the other is data.

I have a knack for figuring out what kind of content will work. I read the data, I see people's reactions, so I know what kind of content can make me go viral overnight. But I'm not comfortable doing that because I wouldn't be proud of the content I came up with. I only make the kind of content that would have improved my own life substantially if I'd watched or read it. The whole objective of my content, whether it's a podcast, whether it's a reel, blog, LinkedIn post, Twitter, or even this book, is I want you to become 1 per cent better than who you were before watching/reading my content.

How can I decide whether you will become better or not? I can only decide whether *I* became better after reading and understanding those things. So, I create content that I feel makes my life better and, in turn, will most likely better yours. This only comes when you are genuine with yourself. If I face a block and you ask me a question and I don't have an answer, then I won't talk nonsense. I won't fake an answer by reading it from somewhere and then tell you that this is my view. That is why I feel like when you are completely honest with yourself and you do something from that place, then there is contentment.

Obviously, you have your lows, you have your ups, and you get frustrated. 'What the hell, man, why is this not happening? I'm putting in so much effort, why am I not seeing growth? Why is my content not going viral? Why am I not able to earn more money?' That's where data comes in.

You need to make rational decisions based on data points (like views, engagement percentages, shares, saves, etc.). Those data points will help you because your perception of yourself is a very different thing from the way the market sees you. The moment you feel that you are above the market, the moment you are away from the market, the moment you isolate yourself, things get problematic—and that is the time you need to look at the data and figure out what you need to do to grow.

But when things are not working out, you have two options. One, you start giving people what they want and become a people-pleaser. The other option is you realize you are one among seven billion people; the phase that you are going through, putting in effort and not getting results—there are hundreds of people like you who are going through a similar situation. If you're going through the same reality that most people are going through, then you are a part of the macroeconomics of the industry, you are a part of the market, you are a part of people.

How would you do something different, something that will help this entire class of people, so that all of you can improve and get through this bottleneck you're facing? When you ask yourself that question, when you choose option two, you start changing things very quickly because you are not isolating yourself, you're accepting that you're not alone, there are millions of others who are facing the same problem, and you start solving those problems. This is when you become a real leader, and you start growing as well because then you are not just accountable to yourself, you are also accountable to your people, your team, your organization. You need to become selfless rather than selfish, and the moment you start thinking that way is when you get mass acceptance and start feeling good about yourself because you'll be making an impact.

Basically, people who isolate themselves from the world get sidelined very quickly. Those who accept themselves and the world around them are the ones who reach the masses. And that's what I do.

You don't need to be intelligent. You just need to be average. Because only intelligent people understand intelligent content; the masses prefer relatability.

So, think in terms of how relatable-y average you can be. The reason why I got to the point that I am at today is because I am the most average and basic young adult you're going to find in India. My story resonates with the maximum number of people because I was born in an average middle-class family, I was born in an average city, and I had dreams to stand out just like an average teenager.

In order to reach the masses, you need to start thinking about how relatable you can be and stop thinking about how you can be intelligent. You don't need to be intelligent to be successful, you just need to start doing things in the most authentic and average way possible. And you need to stay true to yourself.

Key Takeaways

1. Create the kind of content you want to consume.
2. Focus on data to understand what works and what doesn't.
3. You don't need to be intelligent; you just need to be average and relatable.

21

How to Grow on Social Media

Focus on building people and relationships.
Numbers will automatically grow.

Now you'll be like, okay Raj, I IDed my skill, I zeroed in on the expert, now how do I become the best? How do I make tonnes of money off it?

Let's say you love talking and want to become a good communicator. You want to create your own content, build your own podcast, all through content creation and communication. You've identified your skill, the top five people in that field, and you religiously follow them, and now you want to know how to become successful in that field.

You need to understand that there are only two types of people who become successful in today's world. Those who are excellent builders and those who are excellent sellers. You could have a skill that is related to building things. Building teams, building people, building products, building content—you have such talent that no matter what you're given, you'll turn it into something beautiful. Even if you're given the worst team in the world, you'll inspire them and transform them into a unit that works smoothly and efficiently.

Or you're a brilliant seller. No matter what the product, you'll market it in a way that you will sell—and sell loads of it. We've all seen such people—around us or on social media—whose product might be absolute crap, but they sell it in a way that you buy it willingly, because they are great sellers.

So, you are either a builder or a seller, there's no third thing that's going to make you succeed. They're both great skills to have. If you're good at either, you are going to succeed.

Now, you need to learn the core of whatever skill you want to monetize. You need to identify whether you like writing content for other people to deliver or you prefer to deliver something that is written by other people. Decide whether you love building or selling. This is purely based on aspiration. Let's say that you like to speak or deliver content and it doesn't matter to you who has written it, then focus on improving your selling skills. Don't focus on building, or in this case, writing your own piece. Just focus on improving your delivery skills or your selling skills. When it comes to me, I'm a horrible writer, I can't write, so I only focus on my selling and public speaking skills. I'm better than 1 per cent of people at delivery, and that is what has helped me grow.

If you become better than just 1 per cent of others in the same field, you'll make a lot of money. The better you get, the more money you'll make. It starts with being better than 1 per cent, then 10 per cent, then you become better than 99 per cent of others in the field. If you become better than 99 per cent, you become Warren Buffett.

Once you've done this, you only need one thing—distribution. Distribute on all the content creation platforms, distribute everywhere. And if you're good, you will go viral. Don't let anyone tell you that Instagram is dead or Facebook is dead or YouTube is dead or LinkedIn is dead. You will go viral because people are consuming. Do you go on Instagram? Yes. Do you scroll through Facebook sometimes? Yes. Do you check out LinkedIn at least once a day? Yes. Do you watch videos on YouTube? Yes! If you are going on these platforms and consuming content, that means the world is going there as well, and if the world is going there, how can you say any of it is dead? The only thing is that the product evolves.

How do you distribute in a way that gets recognized the most? The one question everybody wants an answer to is how to gain followers quickly. Respect the platform if you want the platform to respect you. So, if you want the platform to recognize you and feature you so that your followers increase, you need to respect the platform.

That means, whenever the platform launches something new, help them build that product by doing that thing more often. The platform will organically push you. Most people grew on Instagram when it launched the videos feature. Others got recognition when Instagram launched stories. People like me got recognition when reels came into the picture. Every time the platform launches something new, respect it by using that feature more than anything or anyone else. The platform will push you. Then, when that thing becomes passé, go with the next new thing. There will always be something new because all the platforms are competing with each other to increase their consumer base. As long as there is competition, there will be innovation. And you'll keep growing as long as you're tapping into every new thing.

As an entrepreneur and as a creator, I ask myself this every single day—what do people want? The answer is happiness. You'll never meet a person who doesn't want to be happy.

Where does happiness come from? Freedom. You're only happy when you have freedom. And there are two types of freedom—financial freedom and emotional freedom. Financial freedom is, 'I'll be happy when I get to do anything I want to do and buy whatever I want to'. It's when you have enough money that you can afford everything you've dreamt about. The second is emotional freedom, which is very, very important, especially in Indian society, because we don't have it. Emotional freedom means, 'I'll be able to make decisions on my own'. I don't need to ask Dad or convince Mom for anything I want to do, be it going to a party or setting up a business. Doing something you want to do without having to ask others is emotional freedom. Now, everything that we buy or do or work on or consume is based on freedom.

That's why we believe in democracy. Democracy is the freedom to choose what we want. And that is why content creation is accepted at large by audiences, as it gives them options and the freedom to choose what they want to consume at different times. Content creation platforms have democratized content and that is why distribution has grown so, so much, and why it will always be in demand. People, when they have choices, will look for creators they relate with.

How is democracy going to help you? Everything you do should help people achieve freedom, make them happy. If you can show people that what you're making is going to give them freedom, they'll fall in love with you and buy more things from you.

Now, the final level is how to persuade people they need your product or service. We are all excellent procrastinators. I can tell you that you need financial freedom and emotional freedom and that I'm going to help you achieve that through my series 'Figuring Out', through my courses on Growth School, through my content on social media, through my book, and you agree that they will help you achieve these freedoms. But why do it now, I'll take a look at it tomorrow, I want to sleep now. This is where the OG level comes. This is what every influencer, every content creator, every businessperson uses to their advantage, and that is urgency.

You need to make people believe that they need your product *now*. How can you do that? By using the two most important emotions. These emotions get you out of bed and make you take action—aspiration or fear. Target these emotions, and you can sell anything to people.

Key Takeaways

1. Either be a builder or a seller.
2. Focus on the quality of your audience instead of the quantity of your audience.
3. Aim for financial as well as emotional freedom.

22

The FAQs of Starting a YouTube Channel

When you shift focus from getting views to giving value, you win.

If you ask a successful YouTuber what their recipe to reaching millions of people is, they will tell you that consistency is key to success. But consistency comes into play once you have started your journey. I will begin from scratch for you guys.

The first and the most significant thing is to find out what you love. If someone is creating makeup tutorials, it doesn't mean you should too. You will never grow if you try to do something you are not good at or be someone that you are not. Create a channel doing what you enjoy the most. If you do not enjoy it, how will your audience? You should feel comfortable, and it should be fun for everyone.

The next step is taking the first step. Just start your channel. For goodness' sake, stop spending days and weeks researching and deciding what you want to do or if you should do it or not. JUST DO IT. Take the first step and everything else will fall in its place. One step at a time.

Now that you have a channel, what are you going to put on it? How long should the video be? Everyone will tell you what you should be doing according to the latest algorithms and whatnot. With attention spans getting shorter, we are told to make videos that are under ten minutes long. But there are videos on YouTube that are an hour long and still have a substantial number of views. What is it then? What should you focus on? Long-form or short-form videos? The answer to this is very simple. Whatever suits you and the topic you are making your video on is the correct duration for your YouTube video. Just because long-form content is working for someone doesn't mean it will work for you too. Your content should add value to the viewer's time. Focus on quality rather than quantity. People will watch hour-long videos if the content is useful and they learn something from it.

So now, you have your content sorted: how do you plan to present it? We all know the power of visual presentation. Everybody has the knowledge but not everyone stands out. Why? Because of the way they convey their ideas. Don't be boring. Your videos should be as entertaining, as informative as they can be. Build your communication skills to keep your audience engaged. Be real. It will help in every aspect of your life.

People starting out with YouTube are generally concerned with the way they should speak in the video.

There have been so many YouTubers who tried to fake an accent when they were starting out, but if you look at their latest videos, they have completely dropped it. The reason being, you cannot fake who you are for a very long time. Speak the way you are comfortable with. I have a formula for this which I call the 'best friends test'. What it means is you should analyse who you are and what kind of person you are in front of your closest friends, how you deliver your stories in front of them, and that is how you should be in your videos, because that is your true self. You being yourself and providing value to people along with it is what matters the most. But don't worry—the style you finally settle on will take time. You start making videos, figure out whether you're being true to yourself and whether it's coming naturally to you or not, and that's how, over the course of time, you develop your unique style.

While we are talking about delivery, one thing to keep in mind is, avoid things that you find annoying in other people or other videos. When you are watching someone's video and wonder what rubbish is this, that is the point you need to cut out of your videos.

Chartered accountant Rachna Ranade has a very successful channel on YouTube. I asked her: How does someone stand out now that YouTube has become so crowded? I could see on her face that she didn't agree with my question. She said, 'If YouTube is something you're doing because everyone else is doing it so you should too, or because you had some extra time to spare, then it will feel very crowded. But if you are really passionate about something and are doing it because you enjoy doing it, then there's still a lot of scope in every field.'

The key, as I said, is consistency. There's always a question of how many videos should I make. And the simple answer to that is whatever you are comfortable with doing consistently. It doesn't matter whether you're doing one video a week or two videos a week—you should just be sure that you can do that consistently. A lot of people will tell you to post content every day. I am not going to offer the same advice. There's no point in taking up unrealistic challenges. Know yourself. Do you think you can commit to posting videos every day? If you can't, don't make that commitment.

Now comes the language in which you should make videos. Many people think that English has been overdone on the platform; so, should you not make videos in English? Choose a language in which you can be your best self. If you are comfortable with English, use English, if you are comfortable with your regional language, do it in your own language. With the growth of tier-2 and tier-3 cities, the demand for regional-level content will increase. So, if you're making videos in your regional language, you can get good traction. You should not switch from English to your regional language because you think English is overdone; switch because there's a good scope for regional-language content in the near future.

Your basics are covered. But is it enough? Is your work done? NO.

The real struggle begins from here. You will succeed only if you practise what I said earlier. Consistency is the real deal. You may have millions of ideas, but if you fail to post a video you promised, then it's pretty useless. Create a schedule. Have a number in mind. If you promise yourself that you will make three videos a week, then do that. Be consistent thereafter. Not a single week should go by when you only post one or two videos. Three videos a week means three videos a week. Take it as God's word, if you are a believer. And honestly, a person who enjoys their work will never find an excuse to go back on their commitment.

In conclusion, do what you love and don't stop doing it. There! This is the secret to success.

Key Takeaways

1. Keep the content true to yourself.
2. Choose the duration based on the topic you're talking about.
3. Algorithms suggest what kind of topics you should do, but it's not set in stone.
4. Try regional content if that's what you want to do.
5. Be consistent.

23

How to Get Over Failure

People are not scared of failure; people are scared
of being 'embarrassed' in front of others.

How to get over failure? The short answer is: there is no other way to get over failure than to get up and get back to work.

It's actually a stupid question: How to get over failure? Do you want to win in life or not? If yes, then get up and start working. If no, then go ahead and sit there, continuing to live the life that you hate and want to change. The ONLY thing that can change your life is action. If you're not going to act, and instead just sit there and think about it, then keep thinking and keep sitting there forever. There is no other way, there are no other strategies or tools or tips to overcome failure. Bro! You want it, you take it. You take action and you do it.

Some people say: I failed because I burnt all my money. Or, I failed because I didn't have it in me. Or, I failed because other people were better than me. I failed because I didn't put in enough effort. So, you KNOW the goddamn answer. Why did you fail? You zero in on that, improve it and start again. You didn't fail because of some XYZ reason, you failed because you didn't know how to win. You failed because you didn't know how to make that thing work. People didn't buy from you because you didn't know how to become better so that people would want you. You are not getting followers on social media because you don't know how to create better content. You are not able to get the right job because you are not prepared enough to get the right job. Learn the skills. You failed in your business because you didn't know how to make the kind of product that people would need or want. So, the question isn't how to get over failure. The question is, *why* did you fail? Figure that out, get better at it and then move forward.

If you think you did everything right and yet you failed because of some external factors, then you need a reality check. 'Life happens for you and not to you'— that's a line by author and speaker Tony Robbins, and it's one I completely believe in. You can't change an external factor, you can't say the government changed, that's why your business failed. Your business failed because your business is so unstable that one political party can decide its future. You say, my entire crypto wallet got trashed because Elon Musk tweeted about it. Yeah! You deserved it. If one tweet from one person is actually decreasing your net worth, then you deserve it. The point is not the external factor, the point is that you didn't prepare yourself. External factors can maybe slow down your process, maybe they can slow you down for a while, but they can't be a reason for your failure. The reason for your failure is you and your lack of preparation.

How to get over failure? This is an extremely stupid question. I hate people who ask me how to overcome failure. You tell me, is there really any other way to overcome failure than to just prepare yourself and do it? I can tell you: No, don't think about it, you're better than this, and fill you up with toxic positivity. But NO! You failed to accept that you were not prepared to get the one thing that you wanted and that's why you failed. You failed in an exam because you didn't prepare, not because you're stupid. Everyone is stupid. The only difference is the rest of them study and pass the exam because of their preparation. You could not clear that entrance exam because some people prepared more than you did. Does that mean life ends there? No! Does that mean you need to go again and do the same thing? No! What it means is that you need to look at life this way: Okay! Listen! *Fail ho gaya toh ho gaya*. But do I really want this thing? If yes, then I'd better prepare for it well and get it. But if not, then I should go and prepare for something else and get that.

You need to realize that if you want something, you have to go ahead and work for it. There's no other way. No matter how many times you fail. The point is—how badly do you want it? A lot of people question whether they should keep doing the same thing again and again even after failing. It's up to you. There's no right or wrong answer. Smart people are those who realize that maybe they don't have the potential for something so they quit and move on to something else. You can do that too. There's no right or wrong in doing the same thing over and over and over again. But next time, when you attempt the same thing, do it having learnt from your past failures; accept that you were not prepared enough for it the last time. And if you decide to move on to a new thing, make sure that you don't make the same mistakes you made earlier, which was a lack of preparation. That's it. Decide what you want badly enough, and work for it.

Your failed attempt will only be celebrated when you become successful.

Key Takeaways

1. It's okay to fail, it's not okay to keep dwelling on it.
2. Figure out the reason you failed, work on it, get over it.

24

The Best Advice I Can Give You

Stop asking people for advice.

The one thing you shouldn't do is ask for advice. Stop seeking advice. People keep asking me for advice. They ask me: What is the one biggest piece of advice you would give me; how can I become like you? They ask for career advice and advice on speaking, and I just want to say— Stop! Because that's the worst thing that you can ask. It wastes your time and that of the person you're talking to.

What is this person going to tell you that you don't already know? Nothing. Because when you ask for 'advice', it's a vague question. What is the best advice you can give me? The best advice I can give you is stop asking for advice. Do you know why? Because there's nothing I will say that would be different from what your parents, your neighbour, or that uncle from that gully who shares his *gyaan* with every passer-by would say.

The point is, if you want to be better, ask better problem-solving questions. If you want me to guide you, ask me specific questions: 'Raj, I started creating content, I have been doing it for the last three months. I'm making reels after reels, I'm on YouTube as well, but even after doing that, even after creating a good community, I'm not able to increase my audience's engagement.' Or, 'I'm not able to reach a point where my audience—who is engaging with me—shares my content so that I can reach more people.' Now, that's a problem, and that's a powerful question that I would be able to answer better than anyone else. You have asked a good question.

You need to have a detailed, specific problem statement so that I have context to what you are asking, what you are doing and where you are stuck. Because until you give me a background and unless you tell me what is stopping you from your goal, I won't be able to help you. Not just me, nobody will ever be able to help you.

Key Takeaway

Stop asking for advice.

25

How to Talk to Anyone

If you don't know what to say, ask questions.

If there is one skill you need to learn, it is how to talk to someone. This is what can make or break any relation in your life, be it personal or professional. You might be someone who loves talking or someone who dreads it, either way you can't deny that it is the most important skill to have. I have got so many opportunities just by approaching someone and talking to them.

So, how do you break the ice? You might say, sure, I can reply to someone when they come talk to me, but even that is scary; or, I don't know how to start a conversation, I don't know what questions to ask; what if I'm bothering that person and s/he is not willing to talk to me? Or I don't know which person to talk to in a room full of people, so on and so forth.

Let me tell you something. If you're scared and are waiting for someone to come and talk to you, that's a losing strategy. You're already scared, you don't know anyone there or if anyone knows you. You have no clue what you are going to do and then somebody comes and asks you something that makes you uncomfortable and you end up stuttering out even the simplest of answers.

That's why I believe you should always take the active approach. You go up to someone and lead the conversation, because that way you get to ask the questions you want to ask and get the information you are interested in.

When you are in a room full of people, the very first thing you need to do is to scan the space. See how many people are busy on their phone or are talking to someone, who are the people who seem rude or annoyed. How many people are shying away from conversations? Which of them don't seem to know who to talk to or what to do? Who is laughing? Who is happy? Who is sad? How many people are selling their products or services and how many people, just like you, are scanning the room? The last kind of people are the best ones to initiate a conversation with. They, just like you, are trying to pick up cues for a better understanding of the room.

Once you have scanned the room and know which people you want to talk to, think about your intent. Why are you interested in talking to them? Are they offering something you want to buy? Are you targeting them so you can sell them something? Do you want them to invest in your business plan? Or is there something peculiar about them which makes you interested in talking to them? Once you know your intent, go ahead and start a conversation.

Two things you need to make sure of before approaching someone: you need to be comfortable, and you need to make the other person feel comfortable as well.

Now that we know who, we go on to how. How am I supposed to start a conversation? I don't even know that person! Great! Go ahead and ask them about themselves. After all, who doesn't love talking about themselves, right? You could try two approaches: open-ended questions or close-ended questions. Close-ended questions have a straight answer. It could be a one-word answer or a binary answer like yes or no. Like, what is your name? Or who do you know here? Open-ended questions do not have a specific answer. These questions give people room to talk.

Now, some people say you should initiate a conversation with open-ended questions. But no! You need to make the other person comfortable first. How do you do that? By asking close-ended questions. Ask them something they don't have to think a lot about before answering. Like, which company do you work for, or what do you do. These questions have a very specific answer.

Your initial question should always make you seem interested in the person. Once a person knows you are interested in them, they become comfortable. And depending on how the person is answering your close-ended questions, you get an idea of whether the person is interested in talking to you.

Once you've made the person comfortable, then you should go ahead with the open-ended question to carry on the conversation. They mentioned what they do or that they work at a particular company? Ask them what they enjoy most about their work or what they find is best about their company. By asking these questions, you have given them room to talk about something that they do and that they are interested in.

But I already asked the basic questions, what else should I ask if I want to continue the conversation? Just observe. What are they talking about? What is something that you need from them? What makes you so curious that you want to talk to them? Or is there something that this person has or can help you with? Based on these questions, you can form your open-ended and close-ended questions. Just observe and ask.

The second thing to pay attention to is your body language. When you show interest in someone, your expressions are animated, your face lights up and the other person can actually see your interest through this. So, talk to someone only if you are actually interested in doing so. There is no point in going up to someone when you are not interested and boring them as well as yourself.

If you want to stand out in the crowd, all you need to do is be positive. Most people are negative: they crib and complain about something or the other and it is ANNOYING. What you should do is to go up to a person and make a positive statement about the current situation. Let's say you're in a Mumbai local and it's crowded and then it starts raining. Most people will start complaining about being late to work, or the roads being flooded. All you need to do is pause, look around, find someone who seems open to talking, go to them and say, 'Hey! I just love rain. I know it's destroying our schedule and we're running late, but it takes me back to the time when I was a kid and I would run out of my house and play in the rain. I used to love that . . . did you do that too?'

By doing this, you are instantly breaking the monotony. You are putting a positive spin on something that the other person is viewing negatively. Now, you've made a positive statement, and if the other person is interested in talking to you, they'll reply, and if they don't seem interested, then you simply walk away. But if they reply with something like, 'Yes man, I used to do that', go ahead with a follow-up question. 'Oh! In Mumbai? It seems to be a little difficult to do that here. I come from a small town, are you from a small town as well?'

BOOM! You started a conversation.

What you are doing here is you're leading the conversation. The positive statement is followed by a close-ended question followed by an open-ended question. You made the first move, broke the ice and led a conversation.

Now you might say, 'Raj, you can so easily make a positive statement. How can we do that?'

Just follow the rule of 4Ws. What are these 4Ws?

Where and what.

You make a positive statement about your particular situation—where you are and what's going on. The rain conversation is an example.

World around us.

This is about the general situation in the world and what's going on around us. Is there something interesting? Let's say you are at a conference and there's a really boring speaker there. Say something like, 'I'm glad they have boring speakers as well because if they weren't here, we wouldn't know the worth of the interesting speakers. Don't you think so?'

Weather.

This is a simple one. Just talk about the weather or anything related to it.

Wit.

I'll tell you a little story. I was once at a conference and saw a girl who was embarrassed and trying to hide because she had spilt Coke on her white dress. I saw that she was very uncomfortable, so I went to her and said, 'You know what? I think you should spill coke seven, eight times more, then it will look like a tie-dye dress.' It is simple wit at an abnormal place about a normal everyday situation which can make the other person comfortable and light. You don't want to make fun of them—they are already embarrassed—instead, you need to try and lighten the situation with a positive statement.

Use a combination of these four Ws and you will never be short of positive statements to break the ice.

The third way to break the ice is with honest and genuine appreciation. When you give someone a compliment that you truly mean, the other person feels really, really good. If you want to make someone like you, you don't have to be a bootlicker or someone who is faking it and trying to butter someone up. That's where you need to focus on the 'honest' and 'genuine' part. You need to figure out what is attracting you towards them and making you want to talk to them. Maybe it's the way they speak, maybe it's their personality, or how they carry themselves and treat others. It could be anything. Be genuine and honest with your compliment and then follow it up with a question.

Now, this giving a compliment can make you come off as a creep as well. When does that happen? When it's about something overly personal. Avoid doing that.

Also, if you want the compliment to lead to a conversation, don't just stick to vague statements. For instance, if you come to me and say, 'Hey Raj, I love the way you speak.' That is a compliment that doesn't move the conversation forward. But if you come to me and tell me, 'Hey Raj, I loved the way you were using voice modulation to make your point. I loved how you used a low pitch and then came to life with a high pitch. How do you do that? Do you think I can do that too?' Now that is an honest and genuine compliment followed by an open-ended question.

DOs and DON'Ts of Giving a Compliment

1. Keep them brief, sincere and honest.
2. Compliment others on what they say and what they do.
3. Don't make your compliment overly personal.
4. Try not to be repetitive.
5. Follow up compliments with a relatable question.

DOs and DON'Ts of Receiving a Compliment

1. Accept a compliment gracefully—smile and say thank you.
2. Don't demean or diminish the giver.
3. Don't assume the person giving you a compliment is trying to get something from you.
4. Do acknowledge the person with a positive comment so that they feel respected.

Key Takeaways

1. Offer value to people.
2. Give a positive statement about a negative situation.
3. Make people feel comfortable.
4. Follow the rule of 4Ws.

26

How a Useless Kid Got to Give a TEDx Talk

The problem with people's mindsets is that they will trust 'old and poor' rather than 'young and rich', because young and rich must have gotten lucky, and old and poor have lived through cycles of rich and poor, so the assumption is that they understand life and money.

Ever since I was a child, I have been labelled as a useless kid. Be it my teachers or the people around me, they all told me I'm good for nothing and will probably end up not achieving anything significant in life. It resulted in low self-esteem and a lack of self-worth. Their tag became my reality.

One time when I was in the twelfth standard, I asked my teacher if I could host the annual school function, to which she replied, and I quote, 'Look at you! You can't even speak one sentence fluently in English, you sleep in most of your classes, how can we afford to jeopardize the image of our school by putting a useless kid like you on stage?' I was devastated, but then I took it in my stride.

As I grew up, I realized I'm not the only one; there are millions like me around the world. In fact, most kids from our generation are tagged as lazy and useless by people who are either older than us or don't understand the way we think. As a result, kids like me often find ourselves feeling powerless and are often depressed about our lives; we tend to get into a zone of self-pity.

Now, for me, self-pity is like a spa. It's okay to stay there for a while, but if you stay there for a long while, it can be very detrimental. So, instead of wasting time staying in that zone, we should latch on to opportunities and—you may be surprised to know this—but the easiest way to do that is by building a network of people.

In my case, I looked up to several influential people from different walks of life and I thought, why not reach out to them directly; that could lead me to better opportunities. So, I became that annoying guy who would stalk these influencers on all social media platforms and expect them to reply. I tried over and over again, but nobody would text back. Even when I met one of them somewhere, they wouldn't talk to me or entertain my questions even for a minute.

Then, one day, I saw this ad on Google. I still remember the text: Attend xx event to explore endless opportunities and build relationships with the world's top leaders. It was for a business networking conference in Mumbai. The next line was 'apply for free', and I was ecstatic till I saw that there was one condition to this offer, and that was 'if you have a business'. I didn't have any business at that time. So, I made myself the founder of 'Shamani Industries' and applied to the conference. And guess what? I got in.

There were about 400 people from different walks of industries at that event. I would approach people and they wouldn't even look at me, and just walk away. There were some people who would talk to me for a while and then would disappear. There was a special category of people: those who would come to me and start selling their products and services and leave the moment I refused to buy anything. The same thing kept happening; nobody valued me enough to give me their time.

And then I saw this guy who was standing in a corner of the dining hall and I went up to him and asked him, 'Why are you not eating anything from this huge buffet?' And he said, 'I was expecting some local spicy food, I don't like East Asian food.'

I was having the same problem, so I immediately said, I know a place where we can get the best pani puri in the city. Why don't we head there?

We went to eat pani puri and talked for a while. He told me he was the president of one of the biggest youth organizations in the country and the founder of three companies.

I was shocked. I asked him, Why are you talking to me for an hour? Nobody in the conference even talked to me for a minute.

What he said went on to become the turning point for me. He said, 'Raj, we are surrounded by people who are constantly thinking about getting more or keep asking for more. In fact, most of the time we become that person who keeps asking for more instead of giving more. So, if you want someone to value you, give them value first. If you won't give them value, why would someone even talk to you? Right now, when everyone was busy selling, you offered me value in terms of pani puri, how could I say no to that? So, if you want to connect with someone, give them something first. Give them a reason to talk to you or value you.'

Boy! That pani puri changed my life and how!

I started researching the people I admired to see what I could do for them. For instance, there was an entrepreneur in Singapore I found inspiring. Instead of texting him to ask, 'Would you help me by telling me how you became successful?' I texted him with, 'I noticed that you are coming to India. Would you like me to help you publicize your tour?' And guess what? I got a reply. In fact, the same entrepreneur later invited me to Singapore to speak with him.

After spending around six to eight months connecting with young leaders, entrepreneurs, influencers and businesspeople, I realized I have built a global network of people from twelve different countries based on just one principle—give.

Now, before writing someone an email, I ask myself three questions. First, what is my intent and why am I reaching out to this particular person? Second, why should this person care and give me even a minute from his or her schedule? And third, authenticity—how authentic is my message? Because, obviously, I don't want to promise something that I won't be able to deliver.

One day, I received a letter from the guy I'd met at the event, and what he wrote was, 'Thanks for the spicy pani puri. I remember you wanted to connect with like-minded people. I hope this will help you.' And attached was an offer letter to do a project with fifty young influencers from thirty different countries in Europe. Oh boy! That pani puri really did change my life.

After that meeting, I never asked for any job, I never asked for any business, I just tried to add value to a person's life while messaging one person a day, seven people a week, and 365 people a year either through social media or email. And that's how I built my network and got the opportunities to expand the reach of my work in more than twenty countries, and also got the TEDx Babson College Talk.

This is how you can add value. Not by thinking about getting, but by constantly giving value to every person you connect with. Imagine a world where the intention is not getting and wanting but of giving to each other.

And here's the secret: one day, one person, one message at a time, for the rest of your life can get you from being a 'useless' person to someone writing a book and telling people how he made it.

Key Takeaways

1. Create your network.
2. Approach one person every day.
3. Every connection you make has the potential to be life-changing.

27

How to Become a
Great Public Speaker

*The way your words make people feel decides
whether you will end up being a leader or a
follower.*

From not being able to speak a sentence in English to
delivering over two hundred speeches across the world.
From being denied a chance to host an event in school to
being the youngest Indian to speak at the United Nations
Assembly in Vienna, and having my own course on public
speaking. I really have come a long way.

Everybody is a learner and then they become a
teacher.

So how did it happen? How did a useless kid get to do
all these things? Well, just like Zuckerberg, it happened
in college.

My experience of being ridiculed in school left me
with no self-worth whatsoever. I dreaded speaking in

front of people. So, when I got to know that I needed to do a college presentation in order to pass a subject, it felt like my worst nightmare coming true. I could hear myself stuttering and my classmates laughing. But I still had one thing. I had thirty days to prepare myself. So, for the next month, I turned on my phone camera and recorded myself giving that presentation. I did that for one hour, every day for the next thirty days. I prepared for thirty hours for a five-minute presentation.

And on D-Day, when I went on stage to deliver that presentation, the entire class, along with my professor, applauded me. I could say that was my Eureka moment, because I loved every bit of it. I loved giving that presentation on stage, I loved the reaction I received, I loved the confidence boost it gave me. And I knew this was what I really wanted to do. My professor even took me around to different classes and asked me to give that presentation in order to show them how a presentation needed to be made. Later, she asked the dean to permit me to speak on stage. I did, and the whole college applauded.

I was so happy that I told myself, now this is exactly what I want to do, and I acted on that. I reached out to all the colleges in my city, requesting them to let me give a presentation on 'How to give amazing presentations' at their institute. Some of them replied, most didn't. Meanwhile, I knew that I wanted to take this to the next level, and for that, I had to get better at public speaking.

So what I did was, I picked up the speeches of speakers I admire(d) the most—Martin Luther King, Les Brown, Gary Vaynerchuk—and started copying them, the exact same pauses, exact same voice modulations, the exact same way of speaking. When I did this with speeches by ten different people, I started to understand how I should speak, where to use a high pitch, where to lower my pitch, everything.

I've put a lot of time and practice to reach the level I am at as a public speaker. There are two rules if you want to become a good public speaker. But before that, you should understand who a public speaker is. If you're talking in front of four people, be it your friends, your relatives, anyone, you're a public speaker. People confuse public speaking with stage performance. Going on a stage and talking or giving a speech is not public speaking, it is a performance.

Public speaking is about how you talk to people in order to influence them and then handle all the objections and questions that they throw at you.

What I am talking about here is public speaking and not stage performance. You won't fail at a performance if you are well prepared. Once you become a good public speaker and prepare well, you will succeed at stage performance as well.

Now, as I said, there are two rules for public speaking.

Rule 1: Never use words that people don't understand.

Rule 1: Ask questions to engage with the audience.

Now, did you see I wrote 'Rule 1' twice? It wasn't a mistake. I never say Rule 2, I always say Rule 1, because all my rules are Rule 1.

So, the first point: did you notice in what you've read so far that I've kept this book simple? That's the same thing I do with my speeches. If you use difficult words, you won't be able to communicate your message to your audience. And for me, it is more important to deliver my message than to use words that are extremely hard to pronounce or understand.

A person who has learnt how to communicate can be a really good public speaker. All of us have to communicate, irrespective of which field we are in. If you are a businessperson, you need to be a good communicator to connect with your customers, inspire your employees and even convince your investors. If you are an influencer, you need to communicate with your audience in order to build a deeper connection with them.

The reason people are unable to talk to someone or tremble at the thought of speaking in front of people is because they are scared of judgement. But what we forget is that *everyone* is scared. Every single one of us. And one way to lessen your fear is preparation. Prepare to put yourself out there, prepare yourself to handle rejections, and work on improving yourself.

Yes, no matter how much you prepare, you're going to falter at some point or the other. Learn from your mistake and convert your goof-up into a story that you can tell an audience.

I follow a framework in order to be a better communicator and a better public speaker. It has everything that I've learnt in these past seven years.

How to get noticed

The first step is to pause. Shhh! You need to stand in front of your audience and just say nothing for a few seconds. The main reason for this is to command attention. Every single human being has an auto-response system embedded in themselves. Let's say I go to a bar, I see a pretty girl and suddenly say, 'Hey! I'm Raj.' The girl will be like, 'Nope!' We see Instagram ads, we scroll past, we see YouTube ads, we skip them. That's our auto-responder working for us. That's why you need to pause and put the ball in the 'Arey, what happened, why isn't he saying anything' mode. You create anticipation. That's how you break the pattern.

So you step out in front of the audience, pause and command their attention. You indicate that you're not going to say a word unless you have their full attention, that they're not doing you a favour by listening to you, you are doing them a favour by speaking to them.

Start with a bang

After you have paused for about ten seconds, start with a bang. If you don't catch your audience's attention in the first few seconds, the men will be daydreaming about women and beer, and the women will be worrying about their loved ones' WhatsApp messages. If you haven't captured their attention in the first ten seconds, then you've lost them for good. So, start with a BOOM! Once, I started a Tedx Talk by playing a guitar and I'm not even good at playing the guitar. Why did I do it? Well, everyone was expecting me to start my talk with a thought-provoking message, but I chose a way that would grab their attention and that they wouldn't quickly forget. Even if they didn't take anything from my talk, they'd still remember me because I broke the pattern and did something that they hadn't expected.

There are four ways to start with a bang.

1. Clichés are a no-no. How do people start their Tedx Talks? By saying something inspirational. How did I start it? By playing a guitar. I don't know if my talk was good or bad, I don't know whether I inspired them, but I made sure that out of the ten speakers that day, people would remember that there was one who played the guitar.

2. 'Yesterday'. Yesterday is a good way to start. Suppose you are at your company's sales meeting. You can't start your five-minute speech playing a guitar. If you start with 'I promise this won't be long, I won't be boring'—the moment you start with these lines you're planting the idea that it won't be that long, but long enough to make them lose interest, it won't be too boring but somewhat boring. Let's say you're in a board meeting and you have to say that last month the sales were good but this month we just couldn't do it. So, you start like this. 'Yesterday I was trying to book a slot on the CoWIN app. I tried everything, my phone was charged, I got the OTP, I put in the OTP, but I couldn't get the slot. That's what I think happened with us. We tried everything to achieve the sales, but we couldn't, and that's just life. But that doesn't mean I'm going to stop trying to get the slot for vaccination. And the sales figures of this month don't mean we are going to stop achieving our sales targets.'

Now, this is such a powerful way to connect with people. You just have to make it relatable. You don't have to think about how you can make it relatable, you just have to talk about yesterday.

'Yesterday I was calling my mom over and over, but she didn't respond. So, I went to her and said, "I was calling you. Why didn't you answer?" And that's what happened with us. We were shouting out loud with our marketing messages, but the customers weren't listening. We need to go out there to every single customer and make them listen to us. That's what we have to do this quarter.' Immediacy and relevance can be built instantly.

3. This is an important thing. Appreciation should be real, not necessary. What do I mean by that? Let's go back to our schooldays. When we had chief guests coming in for any of the functions, the announcement would start with 'Respected principal, respected teachers, respected students'. We all knew there were no respected students there, so that was a formality. That is why you should never start with fake appreciation. There should be delayed appreciation. I appreciate all of you who are reading this book, who took an interest in learning about personal growth. I'm appreciating the fact that you're still reading this book. You stayed even after my boring start, even after my boring stories. That's what I appreciate. You bought this book because you wanted to learn a lot of things. I'm writing this book because this is a part of my personal branding. It's a pure give-and-

take relationship. There's no need for either of us to appreciate the other. Appreciation is something you get beyond what you expected. So, never start your speech with appreciation, it should come in between and be genuine.

4. The last thing is, start with your strength. Everyone has a strength. Mine is rhyming; I love rhymes, so that's what I bring into my speeches in the beginning. Your strength could be anything: your wit, your ability to explain complicated concepts, anything. How to find out what's your strength? It's the way you talk to your friends.

Signature appearance

You should have a signature appearance or gesture. Mine is my whiteboard and marker. You can see the whiteboard and marker in all of my videos. Barack Obama has a signature handshake. Every influential person has a signature gesture that differentiates them from the rest of the crowd. If you want to earn money and fame, you need to come up with something that will be associated with you.

Your one minute of fame

What do I mean by this? Sometimes there are situations where you get only one minute to impress people. Elevator pitch, conferences, you want to impress an employee, you want to impress your boss, you want to impress people on social media, but you just have one minute. This one minute, or even just the first thirty seconds, are going to decide whether you're going to get the next five minutes or not. So how do you prepare for your one minute of fame? The first thing you need to do is understand where you are and what your objective is. And then you start with your strength. You tell people what you have done or what you have achieved. So, I'll start, 'I'm Raj Shamani and I've given speeches in more than twenty-six countries, and I've taught college students as well as the president of Coca Cola, and I have a following of one million people to back this up. Do you want to know how I did that?'

This will either impress them or make them wonder, 'Why is he so cocky, what makes him so full of himself?' In either case, I have their attention now and I have the five minutes that I wanted to get.

It might seem arrogant, but the truth is, I believe in my achievements, and I am bold about it. This gives me the attention that I want. Now I am not asking you to be arrogant always, but to believe in your pitch and in yourself and then, once you have their attention, you can be humble, kind and a nice person who is willing to help.

Now that you have their attention, leave them with a question. Never end a conversation with a statement. Always end with a question and keep people curious so that when they go home, they look you up.

Kiss

Your speech should be like a kiss. A kiss is good when it is short and sweet. If it is really long, it could get suffocating. That's how the message of your speech should be—sweet and simple. The more you try experimenting with it, the worse it will get. The longer you try to stay there, the more your message will get lost. So, how can you make your speech like a kiss? By following the 'less is more' concept. Do not try to add loads of examples; the shorter it is, the better.

The next thing is you need to tell a story, not give a speech. How do you write a speech? You go on Google and copy a few things from here and there and it becomes your speech. If you're going to tell a story, people will connect. If you write a speech, people will get bored.

Now there's a rule that I follow—it's called the 50 per cent rule. No matter what you do, cut it down by 50 per cent. If you have written one page, cut it down to half. If you wrote a ten-minute speech, cut it down to five. I'll give you an example. I can say, 'If I don't evolve on a day-to-day basis, I won't be able to win in life.' Or, 'I need to change myself today.' Most people think the longer the speech and the tougher the words, the better. No bro, nobody has the time. Everyone is busy. So, keep it concise, and you're good to go.

Key Takeaways

1. Never use words people don't understand.
2. Ask questions to engage with the audience.
3. Don't be scared of getting judged.
4. Make the initial few seconds the most captivating.
5. Have a signature appearance.
6. Keep it short and simple.

28

Vision, Mission and the Thirty-Second Rule

You want to get fit? Start with doing a plank for thirty seconds every day. If you do this for thirty days straight, you will automatically be able to do more than that.

You start figuring out where you want to go on day 1 and keep at it till your last day. You should be very okay with, 'I don't know what I want to do but I'm going to do something in my life'. If you have a vision and mission statement for yourself, that's great. A clear vision helps you accelerate the process. But even if you don't, it is completely okay. You should just focus on the next step—what do you need to do right now, right at this moment—rather than obsessing about getting a vision or mission. Don't overwhelm yourself by overthinking; don't stop your progress or stop acting because you don't have that clear idea of what you want to achieve in life.

Think about what you need to do right now, and you take that action and then you keep doing that over a very long period of time. When you are doing it, you realize, okay, this is the one thing for me, and that's when you start accelerating the process. Of course, once you have a clear idea in your mind that this is where you want to be, you can reach it much faster. But in order to reach anywhere, you need to make that start. You need to take some steps. Until you get on the road, how will you start walking? Until you start walking, how will you start running?

In the same way, if you have a mission and vision but don't put in the required work, that would be, well, stupid. What's the point of planning so much if you're not going to actually do anything about it? For those who belong to this category, I have a magical rule for you. A rule that has helped me so, so many times in my life. I call it the thirty-second rule.

Anything that you want to do, anything that you want in your life is just thirty seconds away from you. You just have to embrace thirty seconds of embarrassment.

Thirty-second reels every day grew my following to another level.

Thirty seconds of courage in front of strangers helped me connect with the who's who of the world.

Thirty seconds of reading finance news every day helped grow my money.

Thirty seconds of morning planks strengthened my back.

The hardest thing to do is not the actual work, but to start. And all it takes is thirty seconds. Unable to bring yourself to finish that assignment? Just sit down and work for thirty seconds. Thinking about reaching out to someone? Just accept the thirty seconds of discomfort and send that mail. Scared to go and talk to someone at a conference? Decide to give it a shot for thirty seconds and go up and introduce yourself. I've met so many amazing people just by gathering thirty seconds of courage in front of strangers.

Apply this rule in your life. The initial thirty seconds are the hardest, but if you can get past it, your life will get thirty times better. All your goals will be reached, just through these thirty beautifully embarrassing seconds.

And once you start, keep figuring it out on a daily basis. Goals keep evolving, visions keep evolving, and so do you.

Key Takeaways

1. Be okay with not knowing everything at the beginning.
2. Learn as you go.
3. The hardest thing to do is to start, so start.

29

How to Create Wealth

*You give your time and work to make money, and you
create wealth by making that money work for you.*

How much money you make in life is directly proportional
to the hours you put in at work. But that is not wealth.
Wealth is when you are able to make enough money to
sustain your lifestyle without putting in any effort, time
or skill. It means even if you want to sleep for the next
thirty days, your rent is getting paid. Your bills are getting
paid. All your wishes are fulfilled. Everything's happening
automatically, even if you're not actively making a single
penny right now.

When you don't have to worry about earning money
and you are able to do whatever you want, that is when you
know you have wealth. You have become financially free,
which means you have money in excess of your expenses.
How can you do that? You have to understand that you're
not going to achieve wealth unless you can get other people
to do everything you've learnt. If you have to put in effort

every single day to make money, there will be a day when you won't be able to make money. You need to make money, then you need to start investing this significant amount of money into something that grows automatically, without you putting in any effort. That is why wealth creation is important, that is why investing is important.

Think about it. All of us on an average start working in our early twenties. We work till about sixty with full energy, but after that we won't be able to make as much money as we were making when we were younger. For forty years we make money, and how long do we have to live? Till ninety? So, from twenty to ninety, we only earn for forty years, but have to sustain ourselves for seventy years. After sixty, when we aren't able to make money for ourselves, we'll need to have someone who can make money for us, right? In India, it's called having babies. What you *should* do is start investing in mutual funds, or set up your own company, or invest in other companies and hold equities. Then start putting away a significant chunk of the money you're making through your skills into these investments, so that after sixty, when you stop making money, that creates money for you. This is the absolute gold level of wealth creation.

Think about it this way: if you have to live for seventy years on forty years of income, then how would you live your life differently? Over the years, as your knowledge grows, your money also grows. Learn compounding and use it, or find someone to do it for you. Whatever money you are making, invest at least 20 per cent to 30 per cent of it.

Key Takeaways

1. The amount of money you make is directly proportional to the amount of work you put in.
2. Make your money work for you.

30

The Art of Investment

Invest your time before you invest your money.

This is how I decide on my investments.

I trust in people more than technology. If you tell me there's some person who has some technology that'll change the world, I'll tell you I don't care. I believe in Tata, some other company might have better technology, but I trust Tata more. I trust in a group of people, and that's why I put 50 per cent of my investment money in people who are running good companies. It's not just Mukesh Ambani who is responsible for the success of Reliance Industries. The company has hundreds of people exceptionally well-equipped with knowledge—that's how they're running that company.

So, 50 per cent of the money I want to invest goes into blue chip companies where I feel the management teams are very, very strong. It could be stocks of good companies, it could be mutual funds, all of that. I could also give that 50 per cent of my money to a good financial advisory company and ask them to handle my entire portfolio. This 50 per cent of my money is invested safely, where people have shown great past results, are riding current highs, and have a good vision for the future. They have an exceptional track record because they have been steered by qualified people.

Then, 30 per cent of my investment money is in less safe investments. Again, I trust in people, but with this 30 per cent, I give myself the liberty to take some calculated risks and have a little fun. I go with my gut feeling, my understanding of the market, and my understanding of the economy. I put my money in start-ups when I feel that the person has created an extremely strong company, where the idea is very innovative, and I see the growth potential. Now, from a large group of people—like a management team for the 50 per cent—we have narrowed it down to two or three hustlers and entrepreneurs running a start-up. This 30 per cent I put into angel investing. I get in early so there's a risk-to-reward ratio. As it is said: *Heere ko jaldi tarasho to paisa jyada milta hai.* Sure, I pick up some rocks in the process too, but the returns are high.

The next 10 per cent of my investment money is my fun money. I invest in crypto and uncertainties— who knows when, or if, it will pay off. I gamble with this money and bet on whether the market will go up or down. Even if I face a loss, at least it won't be a huge one. If I were to put Rs 100 in ten years but only get 90 bucks, it's not a bad deal. Alternatively, if that Rs 100 jumped to Rs 200, I'd be happy, as it was just 10 per cent of my money. It really doesn't matter too much either way. I enjoy myself with this 10 per cent.

The remaining 10 per cent I put in absolute certainties, like real estate and insurance. My logic is, if nothing works in life, at least this 10 per cent will.

That is how I invest.

Sandeep Das, strategy consultant and bestselling author, says that, considering the current scenario, the ideal portfolio should be like this: say you're saving Rs 100, 60 per cent to 65 per cent should be in quality debts, because the more you have in safer instruments, the better bets and the better risks you can take. About 25 per cent to 30 per cent should be in two equity classes—large-cap funds and the US stock market. The remaining 5 per cent to 10 per cent should be invested in gold, because it is an excellent diversification vehicle. According to him, the equity market might not give you as much as you think in the upcoming decade. After considering inflation and the LTCG tax, the stock market can realistically give you around 7 per cent to 8 per cent. There are debt instruments which give you that much with no volatility. So, the notion of taking risks and generating returns is actually questionable. The only class of assets which can give you such a disproportionate return is if you have your own firm, because then the return on capital employed can go up to 18 per cent to 20 per cent.

If you invest your money or time in something that is a trend, something you don't know anything about, then it is a bad investment. The hype market is very different from the real market. If we take cryptocurrency, for example, 90 per cent of investors don't know anything about it. No one knows where it came from, what it's about, nothing—people are just following the trend.

Key Takeaway

Take time to understand the market before investing; don't follow trends blindly.

31

How to Invest, for Those Who Don't

You will have to give it time to grow your money, either in finding the right investment product or in finding the right person who can do it for you.

Now the question comes, how should *you* invest? That depends on what kind of investor you are and what your risk-taking capacity is. There are two kinds of people who don't invest—those with decision paralysis and those with loss aversion. The first type of people are those who keep reading and researching and don't end up making a decision. The other type are scared of losing money. They will not invest because of the fear of incurring a loss. Usually, these people have been told not to invest money in stocks. But I know you guys genuinely wish to learn. So, let's talk about how you can come up with an investment strategy.

Analyse your situation and risk-taking appetite. There are three categories—low-risk, medium-risk and high-risk.

Low-risk

A person who has no knowledge about the stock market and cannot risk losing their money should ideally postpone investing till they learn more. Do your research. Watch YouTube videos, listen to podcasts, or better, enrol yourself in a course that teaches investing in the stock market. Meanwhile, Nifty ETFs are a safe choice. Add a small amount monthly and it will give you profits in the long run. Be consistent.

Medium-risk

Medium risk-takers have some knowledge of the stock market. If you belong to this category, you can invest in equity-oriented mutual funds where you get to pick stocks. Work on increasing your knowledge of the stock market. Also, you can look for and invest in products that you believe can be the next big thing.

High-risk

High risk-taking investors can pick individual stocks. It is risky, and if you want to avoid huge losses, then I would suggest you diversify your portfolio. Invest in different sectors. Invest in a systematic manner and you will surely get good profits in the long term.

Aside from this, if you are in your early twenties and don't have enough knowledge on how to invest, then you should let people with the relevant expertise do it for you. Nowadays, there are several apps that you can use to invest. If you don't like to read about investing then just read about these apps and what they do and how they can help you.

The Five Worst Investments You Can Make

Everyone tells you where you should invest your money, but nobody tells you where you shouldn't invest. When we invest for the first time, we do it because someone told us to do so. Be it a bank agent or an individual agent, they try to sell you those products where they get the most commission. It is very important to know what products we shouldn't invest our money in. I'll tell you five financial investments that financially smart people never invest their money in.

1: Regular Mutual Funds
Now you'll be like, 'Bro, everyone says invest in mutual funds, mutual funds sahi hai. So many ads are running, everyone is saying mutual funds are the easiest way to become a millionaire.' Yeah, that's right. Mutual fund SIP is the easiest way to become a *crorepati*; it's when you buy regular mutual funds that the problems arise. Mutual funds are of two types—regular and direct. Regular mutual funds are when you buy a mutual fund through an agent or bank. They get a 1–2 per cent commission but won't tell you about it. A direct mutual fund is when you invest in a mutual fund directly, without using any intermediary. You save on commissions and increase your returns. For example, imagine that after ten years your returns in mutual funds are Rs 1 crore. When you get the money, you would have to pay Rs 2 lakh to the agent. Save the Rs 2 lakh and invest in a direct mutual fund.

2: Product

Product is physical gold. Now you might say that gold is a good and safe investment. Yes, it absolutely is. But if you're buying gold just for investment, then please don't buy physical gold—which means jewellery or brick form. Because, first of all, if you have physical gold, then the fear of it getting stolen will be there. And secondly, it's difficult to know what quality of gold you've been given. Also, when you buy physical gold, there are making charges, melting charges and several other charges which lead to depreciation.

If you have to invest in gold, then do it the smart way—invest in digital gold, or gold mutual funds, gold bonds or buy a gold smallcase, which is the smartest investment in my view. If you compare the returns on physical vs digital gold after ten years, you'll see that smallcase will have given higher returns. Your money is safe, and it appreciates too.

3: ULIP

Bankers will try to sell Unit-Linked Insurance Plan, or ULIP, saying it's a smart investment, but I would suggest you steer clear of it. ULIP is a combination of life insurance and investment. It means that some money will go into insurance and some in assets like equity or debt. On hearing this, you will probably feel like it's a great product, two hits with one arrow. You'll think you will invest in one place and that will cover your investment and insurance too. Amazing! But that's the problem. Let me explain.

When you invest in ULIP, you can't withdraw your money for three to five years; with mutual funds you can do it any time. Sure, you would have to pay some minimal charges, but it can be done. Overall, ULIP charges can be around 5 to 10 per cent, which is very high. In mutual funds, the charges are around 0.5 to 2 per cent. There is very little transparency in ULIP—you won't know every detail about how your account is being handled or where your money is being used. But in a mutual fund, your portfolio is clear, you are aware of every change. That's why I think mutual funds are much better than ULIP.

Now let's compare ULIP with a term life insurance plan. Premium charges for ULIPs fall between Rs 25,000 and Rs 60,000, which are high. Premiums for term insurance plans, on the other hand, fall between Rs 4000 and Rs 20,000 which are affordable. When it comes to life coverage, you will see that it is generally ten to fifteen times your annual premium amount. That means you will get only Rs 10 lakh to Rs 15 lakh, whereas life coverage amounts in term insurance plans can go up to Rs 1 crore, meaning that if you take an affordable term life insurance plan, then that gives Rs 1 crore life coverage. That's why, rather than investing in ULIP, invest your money in mutual funds and term life insurance plans separately.

4: Penny Stocks

Penny stocks means those stocks for which prices are very low, for example, from Rs 1 to 10. People think, 'The price is very low, I can buy one stock for Rs 10, which means 100 stocks for Rs 1000; it's very low and it will increase drastically tomorrow, so let's buy it today for cheap, tomorrow I will be able to earn a lot.' NO. Not every small stock becomes big. You need to remember that if a stock is cheap, there must be some reason why it is so. There must be some reason why the stocks of HDFC, Reliance, Tata are so high, and penny stocks are available for Rs 2 to Rs 5. Why? Because their performance is not good or there is some problem, that's why they are cheap. Try to figure out what that problem is and stay away from such products. Buy the right thing, at the right place and at the right time. Especially stay away from stocks that are less than Rs 10 if you don't know the stock market properly.

5: Lottery or Get-Rich-Quick Schemes

Get-rich-quick schemes are like '*Twenty-one din mein paise double*!' Or 'Come invest some money and become rich overnight'. People sell products like these on the internet—buy this lottery ticket and you will earn lakhs of money. Understand one thing, if you fall for it the only one becoming wealthy is who you're buying it from. You are only becoming a fool.

Key Takeaways

1. Analyse your situation and risk-taking appetite and figure out what category you belong to: low-risk, medium-risk or high-risk. Invest accordingly.
2. It's important to know what products not to invest in.

32

Seven Ways I Make Money

People say you need to learn multiple things to build more income streams, but I believe that you should become an expert in one thing and then build multiple income streams out of that one thing.

You must have heard that if you want to earn a lot of money or create wealth, then you would need to earn through multiple sources. Because one income stream is just not enough to help you earn a fortune. But has anyone told you what these five to seven different streams of income can be? How do you build these sources? How do you earn through these many methods?

Well, I can't tell you this either, because it varies from one person to another. But what I can tell you is today I'm twenty-five and I have seven different sources of income. I can tell you what I did to reach where I am today. I focused on only one thing to create these seven sources of income.

1: Consultancy

Now, what is consultancy? As a consultant, you tell people things they don't know much about. With your knowledge, you help them benefit in some way. Big companies pay good money to consultants.

When I decided on this route, I was a seventeen-year-old kid. What could I teach, at seventeen, that big companies would hire me and pay me for? I was trying to figure it out so I went to my father and asked him, 'What shall I do so that the world will know my value? Tell me some three–four things that I can do which will increase my value.' He said, 'Don't run behind three–four things. Just find one thing and learn it so well that you become an expert at it. When you become an expert, people will regard you as a high-value person, and then you can think of how you can earn money and which companies you can consult with, or what you can do in your own company.' I found that enlightening. I went on Google and looked for skills that would earn me a lot of money, because that's what I wanted to do. But I found nothing.

At that age, kids look for the best courses to join and the best colleges to attend. But instead of this, I searched for 'Which skill will be in most demand in the future?' Then I found out that digital marketing is something that is going to soar, and people don't know much about it. I thought, this is something good. I called some of my friends, talked to them and realized no one knew anything about it, so I went back to Google and looked up 'Where can I learn digital marketing from?' I found out that Google itself gives free certificate courses where you can learn digital marketing in detail, so I did that. I didn't learn all of it, but I did learn one specific thing, which is how Google ads are run. Then I learnt how Facebook ads are run. Now, when I learnt these two things, I had learnt something that many people didn't know, even in my friends' circle.

The father of one of my friends worked in a car company, so I went to him and asked whether I could get an internship in that company. He said, 'No, you're too young.' I said, 'Just tell me some of your problems and I'll tell you if I can solve them.'

So, he told me his problem was with the local dealerships, those who actually sold the cars. They needed to run ads telling people that they now sold this particular brand, but their budgets were low. I asked them what their budgets were. He quoted a number and I told him, what if for half of that budget I ensured that everyone knows about the dealerships?

He first chided me, asking me not to talk nonsense. But I insisted. 'If I do it, give me Rs 25,000. I'm saving you Rs 2 lakh.' He finally agreed, and I then told him about social media marketing and running ads on Google and Facebook and then, because of those ads, people got to know about the dealerships, and this was my first consultancy project.

Since then, I have consulted with many companies about how to grow on social media, how best to sell their products with Google and Facebook ads, and that has become one of my income streams. How much time do I invest in this work? One hour a week. How did I learn it? I did a course, but one course was not enough. I kept on taking courses, and I'm still learning about it today.

Now, when I was doing it, I realized this was a very good skill. One client became two clients, two clients became three clients, till I had six to seven clients and I was still a kid in college. At that time, clients were paying Rs 2000, Rs 5000 or Rs 10,000. They were small amounts, but it made me think—what if I do this on a bigger scale? Even if I am making Rs 500 per person but I'm getting it from 100 people at the same time, it will be a lot of money and the time spent will be relatively less.

Then I got to know about public speaking, and it became my second source of income.

2: Public Speaking

I had learnt social media marketing and how to scale small businesses through social media at cheap prices. So, I started talking about these things in public. In the beginning, I spoke in front of four people, then five people, then ten people, then delivered speeches in many small colleges for free. I used to mail or call them myself, and say, 'I want you to let me speak on stage to your students and I will do it for free. I want to talk to them about how they can earn money through social media marketing in future.' Out of the hundred colleges I contacted, two or three got back saying, 'Okay, since it's free, you can do it.'

I went to those places, and they liked what I said, and through their connections was able to get more such gigs. It kept on growing like this, and I delivered so many free speeches. In fact, the first 100 or so were for free. I went from college to college and said the same thing for free.

After 100 speeches, finally everyone started recognizing my value and I got a call saying, 'We will pay you for it, will you speak to our students?'

So, my second stream of income started.

Now, when I started giving these talks, I observed that, after I would give a speech, the people from there would follow me on social media. At that time, I was not making any content online. I would just post photographs and say where I had been speaking—today I gave a speech in Mumbai, today I gave a speech in Pune, today I gave a speech in Indore, etc. Instagram was new, and I was interested in it. Since I talked about social media, I was obviously on it.

When I noticed people were following me, I saw it as a good sign. I thought, why don't I start speaking on this platform? Because if I go to some place, only a hundred people are watching me. But if I make a video and post it on Instagram, then all the people who are following me can watch this speech and eventually the numbers will grow. I started putting up my talks on social media. I kept on uploading speech after speech after speech for two years. Then I started uploading my content as well, which was not just clips from speeches but specifically made for social media, and after two years, I reached 1,50,000 followers. When I hit that number, I knew that now was the time for a third source of income, that is, brand deals.

3: Brand Deals
If 1,50,000 people are listening to me, then brands are going to be ready to give me money to talk about them

and promote their products. I'm still giving a speech, still talking about the same things, but I'm doing it while wearing branded suits, so that brand would pay me. If I am talking about some bank, they would pay me. Say I am talking about some stock broking company, they would pay me. That's how my third income source started. Meanwhile, my followers increased, till I had 1 million followers. That's when my fourth income source started, and that is, affiliate marketing.

4: Affiliate Marketing

Now, what is affiliate marketing? Suppose I'm talking about a mobile phone and I put a link in the video through which people can purchase that mobile phone. If people click on that link and order a phone, I get a small part of that sale. Say you ordered a Rs 10,000 phone through a link I put up. I will get some Rs 50 because of that purchase. You don't lose anything; for you the phone has been purchased at the MRP of Rs 10,000, but the company will give me Rs 50 because the buyer came through my link. So, this is my fourth income source.

Then I started asking myself, how can I grow on social media? How can I build my own brand? How can I become a content creator? I realized I have an interest in giving speeches about business, about mindsets, about social media. Now since I was thinking and breathing these things day and night, why not start teaching people about it? Due to my expertise in these things, I had four different income streams, so why not make people learn about it too? That's how I started my fifth income source.

5: Courses

I developed a course and priced the ticket for it at Rs 500. So, whoever wants to learn how to speak online and offline and start earning through public speaking can buy my course for Rs 500. People who trust me, people who like my work, people who think that I can teach them something, they can go and buy it, and out of the Rs 500 they pay for it, I give some to my team and my partners, and the money left becomes my income. So, this became my fifth income source. Then people who attended the course said, 'Raj, your course is very good. All the things that you have done and learnt in the last five to six years you have provided in a nutshell in this three-hour workshop. You compressed five years in three hours, you must not have revealed everything, you must have something more.' So, I said, 'All right', and I started writing a book.

6: Book

I signed a deal with Penguin Random House, and now they are paying me to write a book, and this has become my sixth income source. My consulting is going on, my speeches are going on, my brand deals are going on, my affiliate marketing is going on, my courses are going on, and now I've written a book, which will be my sixth income source. I got an advance from the publisher, and how this works is, with every copy sold, I'll get a percentage as royalty. The more the books sell, the more money I will get. And it is not just a short-term thing; whenever a copy is sold, I'll get the royalty.

These were six things. Now, along with doing this, I did one more thing. I started a business.

7: *Business*

People like the content I make and the way it's presented. There is a whole process involved in creating content. I have to decide what I want to say in the video, write everything down, record it, then it gets edited, and I decide when it will be uploaded. Now, whoever wants to become a content creator and wants to tell stories online and make it a lifestyle, they don't need to learn all of it from scratch. They can come to me, and I will give them a video editor, I will give them a script writer, I will give them ideas and I will tell them what works and what does not. I will give them a team that will upload for them too. The team will tell them which videos worked and which didn't and why something didn't work, and to do all of this I take money from them, and the money that I earn from that business becomes my seventh source of income.

So, from one thing, which was social media marketing and how you can grow your personal brand on social media, I created all my current sources of income. I started studying about it in 2014–15, and since then there hasn't been one day, not even one day, where I haven't learnt something new. I research and learn more about this topic every day, and due to that, I have been able to build seven income sources.

Some people come to me and say, 'Raj you did it, great, but nowadays everyone is doing it, so how can we do it?'

Right, everyone is doing it, but there is still a lot of scope left in the field. In today's world, thanks to the internet, tell me one thing through which you cannot make money? Let's say there isn't scope in this area, then pick any other field. The only condition is, whatever it is, you should become an expert in it, because if you're an expert, you can also earn through ten income sources, let alone seven. And you only need to learn one thing, you don't need to learn seven different things for this.

Look at the future, what is the future made of? Technology, Artificial Intelligence. You don't want to learn about that? Learn about finance, stocks. If you don't like that, and you think what I spoke about is really easy, then learn about marketing and social media. Let's say you don't even like that and you only want to speak and earn money through it, you enjoy speaking, then do what I did. First of all, learn about how to speak, how to deliver a speech, how you should do it so that people will want to listen to you. What can you offer so that, after listening to you, people will share your content and follow you too?

Learn about the art of storytelling, the art of social media, anything in which you have interest. It could be coding, it could be politics, music, photography, it could be any damn thing. You grab that one thing and become the best at it, and to become the best you don't need years, you just need the first day. Focus on one thing for one whole day from morning to evening and, at the end of the day, you will know more about that thing than the people you live with.

That's how it begins. On day 1, you will know more than the four people around you. Then you keep learning and you'll know more than the forty people around you. And that forty people will eventually become 4000, then 40,000, then 40,00,000 then 4,00,00,000 and then the whole country.

It all starts from day one. So, pick one skill and start learning and in a few years, you will have seven sources of income and when you have seven to eight income sources, you will be secure. Today, at twenty-five, I don't have any fear of what will happen tomorrow. You, too, won't have the fear of what will happen tomorrow.

Key Takeaways

1. Focus on becoming an expert in one skill rather than running after multiple things.
2. Learn about every type of business and think about how you can apply your skill in them. Wherever your skill fits well, try making money from it.

33

Creating a Personal Brand

*People like people who are like them, or people
who like them; genuinely do both and you will see
millions liking you.*

Your life is your niche. You would have heard me say this
so many times. But it is true to its bones. People who tell
you that this is how you can find your niche, this is the
formula to find your niche, I really don't like such people.
My own friends, when they sit with me for podcasts, they
say this is the model to find your niche and I'm like what
model, bro? Why are you telling someone to be what they
are not?

People think personal branding is about packaging.
People think they need to package themselves into
something that is in demand out there and others will
want to follow them for it.

For me, personal branding is about revealing
yourself, it's about unpackaging yourself. I will only
be able to connect with my audience on a deeper level

when I expose myself completely. This is how Raj wakes up, how he eats, how he sings. Then people will think, 'Oh! Raj is just like me. He also wakes up at four in the evening and then works. If he can make his life like that, so can I. The important thing is to build your life around that. Raj is figuring things out on a daily basis and building his life, I can too.' This is how you connect with your audience. This is how you create a personal brand. When you think about branding, it is about packaging your product. But when you think about personal branding, it is about unpackaging yourself. Exposing yourself is how you scale. Because then you don't need to think about how you have to speak in front of different people or how you have to present yourself differently around different people. You don't have to think about any of it because you will just be who you truly are.

I don't have to talk just in English or Hindi, I don't have to wear fancy clothes, I don't have to stick to my niche, because I am my niche. If you look closely, even the biggest brands, whether in India or the world, are their truest self in front of the camera, that's why they have the biggest audience.

To get something from your personal brand, you need authority. How do you build authority? By adding value to people's lives. How do you add value? By either entertaining, inspiring or educating someone. How do you do that? By just putting out what you are doing and helping other people find the answers that you are trying to find out for yourself. Because you are your own niche.

For example, you want to be the greatest writer in the world and you are trying to figure out how to get there. Whatever you learn, you try to experiment with in your life, whatever works, you share it with other people as entertainment, inspiration or education. Once you start doing that, other people will start applying your learnings in their lives, and once they apply those learnings and see results, they will consider you an authority, and when you have that authority, you've built your personal brand in front of them.

Branding is about trust. At the end of the day, I am doing something that ten other people are also doing. But I'm providing it in a much better way so that people now see that they're getting more value out of me. When they see that, they're going to differentiate me from the other speakers: Raj is much more brutal and real than the others. So, everyone is a speaker, but how do you identify someone who speaks honestly? You tag them as Raj.

There are hundreds of Rajs as well. How do you differentiate between them? Then Raj becomes Raj Shamani. That's what a personal brand is for me. That's the tag of trust. You build trust by continuously providing value in people's lives. When you do that, people consider you an authority—and until and unless you are an authority, they won't trust you.

Key Takeaways

1. You are your own niche.
2. Build trust in order to build a brand.

34

Creativity and Growth

Nothing happens with talent; the game is only about consistency. Consistent effort = Consistent growth.

All through my school, all through my life, I tried so, so many things. One thing I got to know about myself is that I'm not creative at all. I'm the least creative person around. The only thing I know, the only thing I am a master of is discipline. When I'm making content, I rarely go, 'Oh! I have got this amazing idea and I am going to make a new product around it.' No. All I know is, today, at 6 p.m., a reel has to go up. If I don't have it ready yet, then I have to make it. It doesn't matter what I'm going to make, but I know I'm going to make something. I force myself to create, I'm not a creative person.

When it comes to business, I apply the same discipline. When the pandemic hit, my usual products were put to a halt, and I knew I had to make new products in order to sustain my business. I didn't have any amazing ideas that I knew for sure were going to work. So, how was I creative about building a product that would actually work?

I started with sanitizers, because that was the need of the hour. Now, I had to decide between premium and low-priced. I decided to make it premium and launched a disinfectant spray. Soon, I realized I would have to make a low-cost product as well because the premium range only had a limited market. So, I launched a toilet cleaner. Once I launched the toilet cleaner, I realized homes need floor cleaners as well, so I launched that as well, because most people buy toilet cleaners and floor cleaners at the same time. And then I thought, let's launch a handwash too.

So, in six months I launched five new products. Out of these, I stopped three, and the other two products are still working well. If I had just sat around thinking how I should creatively make a product which has a nice bottle, smells good, and can beat the existing brands, I would never have been able to launch any product.

I don't have creativity, I have discipline. If I have to launch a new product this month, I will. I don't know what product I it is, but I will make it. I don't know what reel I have to post today, but I will post a reel. I have discipline that forces me to keep on creating. And as I keep creating, my bar keeps getting set higher—I want to create something better than what I created yesterday. I keep on doing that every single day, so at the end of the tenth day, whatever I create is going to be better or more 'creative' than what was done on the first day. It is going to be an improved version of my original idea. This is how you can be creative too—by creating on a consistent basis.

Do you have a basic sketch of an idea? Go ahead with it. Start creating, start posting, take people's feedback, see how you can improve, post the improved content the next day and keep repeating the same steps. As you keep creating, you'll keep improving. You just need to be better than who you were yesterday. That's it. Do that, and it will be a game-changer.

Key Takeaways

1. Build systems to keep you consistent and that will force you to get better.
2. There is no one talented enough who can't be beaten by consistency.

35

Growth

You know how to achieve 50x growth in a year?
By growing 1x every week.
Think of growing 1 per cent every day, instead of
100 per cent in one day.

When you start hustling early in life, you don't have to worry about whether you'll be able to pay rent tomorrow, and it gives you a certain peace of mind. Sure, some things take more effort, some take less effort, but once your business is set up, the struggling period is over, and then you just enjoy it.

Most people don't do anything in their life because they are comfortable. The biggest step they have to take is leaving that comfort zone. Sure, that is a big step, but the life you live after is worth everything.

I've always been a pampered child. Growing up, I didn't have to do anything on my own, I never had to make my own bed, never had to clean or anything. Then I chose a career in public speaking and with that too I was very comfortable. I stayed in luxurious hotels and that meant I didn't have to do anything myself.

In early 2021, I decided to move to Mumbai, and then I had to do all the little things on my own. These little things keep you organized and give you a sense of responsibility; you know that there are things that need to be taken care of on an everyday basis because, if they aren't, you're going to have cockroaches in your home. And this is something you need to apply to all aspects of your life. If you don't put in effort every day, things will rot. So I learnt a lot after coming out of that comfortable bubble I was living in. The only reason I did it was because I knew I wouldn't be able grow as much if I stayed in my comfort zone.

Earlier, I was someone who wouldn't share another person's content when I thought it was good. I would wonder why I didn't think about this first? And I'd hope that others wouldn't watch that content. This was because I felt inferior. When he realized that I felt inferior, my dad tried to help me overcome it, not by buying me things but by making me more confident. Now, this new Raj shares every good thing he comes across. Now, I take inspiration instead of getting intimidated.

See, I still think 'why didn't I make this' when I see someone posting something good. But now I also think, 'This is great, and I'll be inspired by you. Your good content will push me to do better myself. I don't care whether you have 300 followers or 300k followers, I'll still post you. I don't care whether you are a small creator or a larger-than-life brand. I like your content, I'll share it.' It gives me a reality check—Raj, there are others who are making better content than you and if you don't up your game, you'll cease to exist. If I need to move forward, I need to make great content like this.

There's no space for jealousy in my life anymore, there's just inspiration and growth.

Let me tell you a secret tip to grow: whomever you're jealous of, start promoting them. Now, there are two things: one, it takes A LOT OF effort to promote someone, and two, you feel better about yourself when you do it. You feel that you are becoming a part of this person's journey; it may be small, but you are a part of it. Once you start doing this, you automatically get into the give, give, give mindset, and that's a game-changer.

Give, give, give so much that the other person feels guilty and will give you something in return.

Key Takeaway

Since childhood we have been taught, if you have taken something, give something back; use this to your advantage. Give to people up front, so they always feel like giving something back.

36

Why I'm Unbeatable

*Your audience will move on if you don't give them
new reasons to stay every day.*

Everything I do in terms of my content creation comes
from my business. Let me explain through examples. If
you look at my content, you'll see that I am constantly
searching for my Product-Market Fit (PMF). Anyone
who understands the start-up world knows that this is
what people are trying to zero in on. So, what does this
PMF mean? It's when a product finds demand in the
market—it fits the market and becomes successful. For
instance, you come up with a product which is in demand
in a particular region or platform. You give the market
exactly what it wants, and it will blow up.

In India, when TikTok got banned, Instagram
spotted the opportunity and launched Instagram reels.
Instagram decided that whoever makes TikTok-like
content on Instagram will be given a lot of reach. So,
the entire TikTok crowd moved to Instagram. Now, the

market was ready and the demand was there. All I did was launch a product to fit this demand. At first, I tried to keep my speeches to thirty seconds, but that didn't work out. Then I started making coffee and stuff, but that didn't work out either. So, I decided to show my sneakers and, no shocker, that didn't work.

I thought, leave all this, I will do what I do best. I provide information in easy-to-understand terms. I read the news daily and no one is talking about it, so I will talk about it and people might like it. I did three business-news reels. The first video did okayish and the second one too. The third video blew up. So did the fourth. Then the fifth. And I saw that this was my product-market fit. So, with the help of an entrepreneurial mindset, I had experimented and adapted till I found my PMF.

Here's the thing: creators need to reinvent themselves constantly, or else people are waiting to steal their audience from them.

Now another thing: once you get your product-market fit, all you need to do is scale. So I made a system for myself. I used to wake up, go to the washroom, and while I was there, I'd read the news and pick up three things for that day. I would come out, make the video and upload. And within ten minutes my whole day's work was done. Now the rest of the day was only about—what's next? I experimented with more content. I introduced finance, then I introduced mental health, then public speaking— everything following the 'three things' concept.

Now, when I started to grow, a lot of competitors came into the picture. Even the big creators whom I admire a lot started copying the 'three things' format. What do you do when competitors come in? You either scale up so much that they can't touch you, or you improvise and pivot to different things.

I scaled up for a month and started posting multiple videos a day. But I realized this wouldn't work and I needed to pivot—go in another direction instead. So, what I did was, I brought my public speaking back into the picture because now I had an audience. Then, I pivoted from there as well and went into an angry, shouting mode, because everyone else started speaking slowly as well. Then I moved to rap (see my high school hustles finally paying off?), and I started using rhyming words. Then I found my product-market fit again and I started with extremely slow and conversational content. Now, all this I have learnt from the business world. You need to constantly pivot so that you can actually nail the market and sustain the audience that you have built.

Another thing that I learnt from the business world and applied in my content was that you need to build your moat. What is a moat? Have you seen old forts and castles? They have a body of water surrounding them. A gate in the fort opens up and acts as a bridge across this water, and as soon as people enter, it closes. Until and unless that gate opens, no one can enter the fort. That moat is to stop people from attacking the fort. So, build a moat and guard yourself so that other people can't come and attack you. I told myself, Raj, you need to find your moat. Every start-up has a moat. Some people have technology, some people have money, so what is my moat? My moat is that I can break down any complicated topic and present it in an easy-to-understand manner because that is what I have been doing for the past seven years of my public speaking career. BOOM. That worked out. The first video I did based on this concept blew up. It reached 30 million views. It went mad viral.

Now that that happened, the other business lesson comes in. How do people remember you? What are your brand guidelines, so that whenever someone sees something they instantly remember you? That's where the whiteboard, the marker, the mic placement and different camera angles come in. I did it so much that people started telling others to copy my style. Now that is my brand guideline. And if you guys remember, each of my reels ends with a *doom* sound. Sometimes the message might not be complete, the last word might be cut, but that *doom* won't be cut. That *doom* is my logo, my signature, my audio branding.

Now comes another business-world lesson. Every business has a vision. Content creators don't have a mission or vision. But I have a vision—I believe that people know what they want to do; all they want is for someone to remind them from time to time. Raj Shamani is your daily reminder. I am that reminder for you. You know what you want to do but you need someone to remind you. So I'm going to come to you every day and remind you, 'Hey! Listen, you are better than who you were, you don't need to be jealous, you are comfortable, you can do this.' I just tell people basic things.

So now that I've set up these things—when I created a vision, set a guideline, pivoted, created a moat, when I decided on my signature and audio branding—now that there are so many things combined in making my content, it is very difficult for anybody to come and beat me.

Key Takeaways

1. Creators need to reinvent themselves constantly.
2. When there is competition, you either scale so much they can't touch you or you improvise and pivot to different things.
3. Create personal brand elements, so whenever someone sees something associated with you, they instantly remember you.

37

Stand Out from the Competition

When you work hard on something you're passionate about, money is a byproduct that will show up at your door sooner or later.

Do you think of competition as a roadblock? A villain in your life of dreams? As a hurdle to your becoming successful?

I'm going to give you a concept, a mental model that will help you eliminate most of your competition.

I call this concept the Circles of Life.

So, imagine the whole world as a circle. Now, create multiple circles inside of it to represent different fields and niches that people work in.

Now, identify your place in it by following these steps.

1. Figure Out Your Interests
When I realized my deep interest in start-ups and businesses, I knew it was something that I should pursue,

because a normal day for me was spent on websites like CrunchBase, MoneyControl, Forbes, etc.

So, keeping your interest in mind, you will eliminate the first set of people from your competition. Your first circle.

2. Figure Out Your Strengths

What is that one thing about you that can help you gain leverage in the crowd? It doesn't have to be an obvious 'entrepreneurial mindset' or 'hard-working nature'. It could be as simple as being a good listener, an observer like me or a people person.

This is the quality that, when combined with your interests, will guide the career path you want to take.

After I realized my interest in start-ups, I used the strength of my curiosity to start the *Figuring Out* podcast.

Similarly, once you know your interests and strengths, you can eliminate another set of competition by reducing the size of your circle.

When you know your strengths and interests, you look around to find that most people you thought of as competitors are not even in the game now! They either have different interests or different strengths.

Is there a way to further reduce competition? Yes, there is. It might be a little cumbersome to work on, but it's effective.

By now we know that to decrease competition, we need to decrease the size of our circle. Now, how do we further do that?

By being more specific in our approach.

So, let's say once I knew that I wanted to start a podcast about entrepreneurship, I still had to compete with a lot of other podcasts around the same topic. I removed myself from the competition by adding just one more thing to my roster: interviewing 100 unicorn founders about how they built their businesses.

This made *Figuring Out* stand out as a podcast, and now we rank number one in the entrepreneurship charts.

You can look at any successful creator who has grown recently and see how they eliminated their competition.

Sharan Hegde from *Finance with Sharan* is one of the many finance creators that boomed. But why is he the biggest right now? It's because he eliminated competition by being specific and elaborate with his target. He started sharing financial knowledge on Reels, which were funny and had a unique format. You can spot four circles here.

Similarly, Tanmay Bhat leveraged his sense of humour while he was streaming with popular gamers and comedians, and then applied his business acumen to build a content empire on YouTube. Another four circles here.

A lesser-known name is Shaurya Shikhar. Shaurya is one of the most sought-after people on YouTube in India. He works with big names, including BB Ki Vines and Ankur Warikoo. The reason why he doesn't have competition is that he became an amazing data analyst for YouTube and publicized himself through threads on Twitter. Yet again, four circles and minimum competition.

Just like all these people, you have to start looking for your circles. Interests and strengths are going to be the most basic, and they will eliminate a lot of competition. But you will still have to figure out more ways to further reduce this competition. It could be your platform, medium, language or style.

After this filtration process, you will know what you want to work on, and there will be limited competition as well.

Key Takeaways

1. Use the circles of life concept to identify your niche.
2. The more specific you can get with your strengths and interests, the more you can eliminate competition.

38

Short-Term or Long-Term?

*If you want to make money, work on the things
that are trending today; but if you want to become
filthy rich, work on things that will be trending ten
years from now.*
*Everyone who has become a billionaire has done
so by playing a game that will be relevant ten
years on. Mark Zuckerberg started building a
social media platform years ago, Jeff Bezos started
building an e-marketplace years ago, that's why
they are rich today. They invested in the future and
played a long game, a very long game.*

There's no doubt that our generation expects instant gratification. We want what we want and when we want it. Is this good or bad? Well, it depends on your intent. You can do whatever you want, have whatever you want if you have the right intention. Now, you'll ask me, Raj, what defines the right intent? I'll tell you. You see someone the same age as you, from a similar background, but doing better in their life in some way, and you would like to be in the same place they are. Or your ex broke up with you and now you want to be successful just to show them what they lost. Though you are trying to improve your life, you are doing it for the wrong reasons.

Let's take an even more simple example. Let's say you earn Rs 20,000 a month and you want to buy an iPhone. Now, if you want to buy an iPhone because you really want to and you think it'll make you happy, by all means, go ahead, buy the phone on an EMI plan if you want to. That's why we have EMIs. But if you want to buy an iPhone because you think it will increase your social status or because your friends have it or because your favourite content creator has it, then STOP—that right there is the wrong intent. That is when you need to let go of the instant gratification mentality and think about the long term. Do something because you want to do it, not because someone else is doing it.

Now, in my case, my FMCG business was my instant gratification, and my content creation was a long-term goal. Moving from my FMCG business to being a content creator was a big step for me. I was moving from an established business that I knew would grow more than content creation would. But I also knew that after six years of creating my personal brand, the reward I'd receive in the seventh year would cover all the losses I'd incurred so far. And that my personal brand would also help me scale my FMCG business to a level I otherwise wouldn't be able to reach or would take me significantly more time to reach. I got so many deals for my FMCG business because people wanted to work with me as a brand. So, whatever I'm creating is going to help me reach the level I envision for myself.

That is my short-term goal. My long-term goal is to create a community. When I started, no one supported me. So, I decided to build a community through which I can support everyone. I never say no to anyone who is trying to do something new. If I see that their intention is good, then I give everything I have to help them grow. I give my time, my reach, my distribution, my brand, I give my money, anything that is needed. This is the reason I'm becoming a creator and expanding my reach, so that I can be a crucial part of the Indian growth trajectory, where we can build and nurture young start-ups and take them to a global level. I don't want any start-up with good potential to struggle for five years to reach the one-million point like I did. If our values align, I'm ready to provide my one-million reach to someone and help them grow. Because when they grow, I believe that I am growing.

As I said earlier, thirty seconds can change your life. What you do in the next thirty seconds of closing this book is going to decide the next thirty years of your life. Once you finish this book, decide your short-term and long-term goals, and start working on them.

You have self-doubt? Do it anyway.

Feeling anxious? Do it anyway.

Feeling scared? Do it anyway.

If you want to get somewhere in life, you have to do it anyway.

Because if you don't do something, you'll be stuck.

And trust me, worse than self-doubt, worse than feeling you are not enough, worse than feeling inferior, is the feeling of being stuck in one place.

Key Takeaway

Decide on your short-term and long-term goals and start working on them immediately.

39

Things I Wish I Was Taught in School

Ten Things I Wish I Was Taught in School about Finance
By Sharan Hegde (management and investment consultant)
Instagram: @financewithsharan

1. **Asset Allocation**

   The stock market has historically been the best-performing asset class beating gold and debt by a huge margin. So, for long-term goals (>seven years), logic would dictate that we should invest all our money in equity instruments such as stocks and equity mutual funds.

   Over the past thirty years, 100 per cent equity investment was only 0.4 per cent better than an equal allocation strategy across equity, debt and gold, but at the same time it was twice as risky.

   Research conducted by Capitalmind found that a simple equal allocation strategy, i.e., 25 per cent

Indian stocks, 25 per cent US stocks, 25 per cent gold and 25 per cent debt, showed 14 per cent compound annual growth rate (CAGR) over the past thirty years but with half the risk. Meaning for only a 0.4 per cent reduction in CAGR compared to the 100 per cent investment in Indian stocks mentioned above, the risk reduced by half.

Thus, asset diversification is paramount to improve our risk-adjusted returns and quality of sleep at night. The research further goes on to say that the best asset allocation for long-term investing, such as retirement or financial independence, is 50 per cent Indian stocks, 25 per cent US stocks, 15 per cent debt and 10 per cent gold.

2. **Life Insurance**

Before investing even a single rupee on mutual funds or stocks, it is important to take care of two things—health insurance and life insurance. Out of the two, the amount required for life insurance can be a little tricky to calculate because, unlike health insurance which only takes care of medical expenditure, life insurance needs to account for our entire lifetime value which would incorporate our lifestyle, future plans, dependents, liabilities, etc.

Purchasing a simple term insurance policy is the most economical and smartest way to purchase life insurance. Avoid money-back policies such as endowment and ULIPs since they have very high premiums.

Having said that, it might also be a good idea to purchase 'riders' or add-ons to our term insurance policy to cover exceptional circumstances. The most popular riders are explained below:

Accidental death: If you pass away due to an accident, your family gets an additional amount over and above the basic policy. This rider is usually taken by people who work in hazardous environments like factories or by people who travel frequently.

Accidental disability: If you are partially or completely disabled due to an accident then you get paid a certain percentage of the sum assured over five to ten years.

Critical illness: If you are diagnosed with a critical illness like cancer, or have had a heart attack or are paralysed, you get paid a certain amount of the sum assured.

3. **Health Insurance**

   Get an insurance policy with restoration benefits especially if it's group insurance with your family.

- Avoid policies which have a limit on room rent.
- Avoid policies which have a co-payment clause in it.
- Prefer policies which do not have disease-wise sub limits.
- Prefer policies which have day-care treatments covered.
- Purchase policies with less waiting period, such as one or maximum two years.

4. **Investing in Gold**

   From an investment perspective, purchasing physical gold jewellery is the worst way to go because you lose 12 per cent of its value as soon as you walk out of the store due to 'making charges'.

The best option is Sovereign Gold Bonds (SGB) issued by the RBI. We can purchase up to 4 kg of gold bonds per year. They are issued in denominations of 1 gram, and hence are affordable to most middle-class investors. Gold appreciates at 6–7 per cent every year. SGB also gives a 2.5 per cent interest rate on top of this. This way, the effective returns turn out to be 9–10 per cent.

The tax treaties of SGBs are very investor-friendly. The capital gains component (i.e., tax on the normal 6–7 per cent appreciation of gold) is completely tax-free and is held until maturity of eight years. The 2.5 per cent interest rate is disbursed semi-annually and is taxable as per income slab. The post-tax returns overall are still lucrative enough to make it an essential requirement of our portfolio.

5. What Is Money?

The world revolves around money. But have you ever stopped to think and ask yourself what exactly is money? The most common definition is that money is a medium of exchange. But what exactly is being exchanged?

The answer: TIME.

The only valuable asset that every person on this planet has is the twenty-four hours we get every single day. It's like businessman and author Kevin O'Leary says, 'Salary is the drug they give to make you forget your dreams.' To test this, simply ask yourself if you would go to work every day if you had all the money in the world. Most likely the answer would be 'no'. All of us have other unconventional goals and aspirations which we would like to explore before our time is done on earth. That's why financial independence is so important. Otherwise, you will work for the rest of your life for people and companies who have achieved financial independence.

6. Education Loans

The interest rate parity concept states that the interest rates in different countries cannot be compared on an apple-to-apple basis.

Let's take an example to understand this better. Let's say you take a $100k loan at a 10 per cent interest rate from both a US and an Indian bank. This is roughly around Rs 80 lakh (assuming $1 = Rs 80). Let's assume that the repayment period is three years. In those three years, the rupee would have depreciated against the dollar to an average of Rs 86 (Rs 80 to Rs 92). Also, the loan amount accumulated including interest would be $132k or Rs 1.05 crore. Now, when you repay the US bank, you have to repay the entire $132k. But when you repay the Indian bank, you have to repay Rs 1.05 crore/Rs 86 = $122k. See the magic? You save $8,000, which is about Rs 6.4 lakh. If you consider a longer repayment period, the savings are even more.

So, that's why a 10 per cent interest rate US loan is not equal to a 10 per cent interest Indian loan. It's actually equivalent to a 15 per cent interest rate Indian loan. Opt for a US loan only if the difference in interest is greater than 5 per cent.

7. **Psychology of Money**

   MRI studies have shown that the act of paying stimulates the same part of the brain involved in processing physical pain. Hence, the time duration of paying for an item plays a significant role in determining our spending habits. When we pay for something in advance, we are far more likely to enjoy the item as opposed to paying for it while consuming it.

   This psychological bias is what brands leverage upon to alter our purchasing behaviour. Amazon and Uber gift cards are prime examples of this tactic, where we are asked to pay a certain amount in advance with the lure of 'CASHBACK'.

   When the time comes to actually purchase the product or consume the service, we do it guilt-free since the pain of paying has already occurred in advance, thereby reducing 'checkout friction', which happens to be the biggest friction point in the purchasing cycle.

   In the process, we are also likely to spend more than we are accustomed to, since the pain of paying has been eliminated altogether.

8. **Tax-Saving Strategies**

   A home loan is most likely going to be the biggest loan of your life, which would last for twenty to thirty years. During that period, the government gives us multiple avenues to reduce the cost of home ownership through tax breaks.

   The law states that you can utilize up to Rs 2 lakh of the interest payment in a year to reduce your taxable income. Also, you can utilize up to Rs 1.5 lakh of the principal component in a year to reduce your taxable income. Thus, the total reduction becomes Rs 3.5 lakh.

If you're in the Rs 10 lakh+ income bracket, then that implies a savings of 30 per cent of 3.5 lakh = Rs 1.05 lakh every year. You can double this tax savings if you co-borrow the home loan with your spouse or family members. Hence, it becomes very tax efficient to take a joint home loan, especially when there are multiple working members in the family.

- Caveat for interest deduction: Cannot be used when home is under construction.
- Caveat for principal deduction: Home cannot be sold within five years, else tax savings will be reversed.

9. **Credit Card**

   A lot of us are clueless about the mechanics of a credit card when we first get one. It may seem like a simple tool that enables us to spend money and pay later but there are certain nuances which we need to be aware of to avoid hefty interest expenses.

   One of the jargons which deceive a lot of us newbies is the 'minimum amount due'. This amount is usually 5 per cent of the credit outstanding. If you pay only the minimum amount due, you avoid getting tagged as a defaulter and maintain your credit score, but it leads you into a spiralling path of credit debt. No other lending product comes close to the sky-high interest rates charged by credit card companies—they charge 2–3 per cent per month (~40 per cent annualized).

Also, if you're paying only the minimum amount due, the interest gets calculated on a daily basis from the day of transaction. Meaning, even if the payment was due five days back but the purchase was made twenty days back, the interest would be calculated for the entire twenty days, and not five days. However, if you had paid the entire amount due, the interest would be zero.

If you're unable to pay off the entire amount due, it would be better to convert it into a low-cost EMI, balance transfer or personal loan.

Another thing about credit cards is the CIBIL score. It is a score that represents your credit worthiness. It ranges between 300 to 900, the higher the score the better. A higher CIBIL score gives you benefits like low interest loans, better car insurance, etc., whereas a lower score may result in rejection of credit card or loan application.

How can you increase your CIBIL score? Here are some tips:

- Ensure you spend only 30 per cent of your credit limit per month.
- Ask your bank to increase your credit limit. You need to show that despite having a lot more credit, you keep your utilization low, thus improving your score.
- Get a secured card against a fixed deposit and repay the balance on the due date.
- Avoid being a guarantor of loans or having a joint account because any default from the other party will reduce your score.
- Have a good credit mix of secured and unsecured loans.
- Pay on time.

10. Investing in Stocks vs Debt

Why is it so hard to convince ourselves to avoid investing a bulk of our net worth in fixed deposits? This is because of something called 'risk aversion'. Most of us cannot fathom the fact that investing in the stock market entails a probability of losing a part of our principal investment. Even though the probability tends towards zero over a 7–8-year horizon, we are unwilling to invest our hard-earned money unless it gives guaranteed returns.

But we don't realize that putting all our money in 100 per cent assured zero-risk investments such as fixed deposits is a sure-shot way of guaranteeing negative real returns after considering tax and inflation. Even though we see the absolute number increasing year over year, the purchasing power of our slow growing money decreases. It will take us significantly longer to achieve our financial goals, if we ever reach them at all.

Hence, it is important to allocate a certain portion of our portfolio towards riskier asset classes such as equity, to ensure real growth in the value of our overall portfolio over a long-term period. Even though there is a probability of facing short-term losses, it is imperative to build the financial discipline to stomach those losses and understand that it's part of the process which would eventually lead to real growth in the value of our wealth over a long-term period. Taking no risk at all is also a kind of risk, which we don't realize until it's too late.

**Nine Things I Wish I Was Taught in School about
Growth and Marketing
By Vaibhav Sisinty (entrepreneur)
Instagram: @vaibhavsisinty**

1. **Generating Traffic from Search Engines like Google**
   In today's world, it is very important for kids to
   understand how search engine optimization works.
   Why a particular bakery shows up when you search
   for bakeries on Google, and what role content plays
   in it. If students know how basic SEO works, they can
   start creating content and drive traffic very early on.

2. **Power of Content Creation and Building a Personal
   Brand**
   Personal branding means how you can create content
   about everyday things that you are learning that other
   people will be interested in consuming. For example,
   if you are someone who loves creating handwritten
   notes for yourself, you can make it shareable with
   other people with an interest in the same subject
   matter, and project yourself as an expert in that
   particular domain. You can do this through blogs,
   short videos, etc.

3. **Understanding Numbers and Analysing Them so
   They Work for You**
   So much of the math we learn in school or college
   feels almost inapplicable after we graduate. If we
   were taught to understand numbers and build
   correlations, that would make us analytical thinkers
   and help us more in the long term. If math were

taught in a more real-life scenario, it would become way more powerful. If you can teach yourself how to understand the numbers, like how many impressions you got, how many likes, if there is any correlation between the impressions and the number of likes, etc., that would be very useful to you.

4. **How to Make New Friends and the Art of Networking with People**

   Something I was never taught was how to make friends and network with people. It is one of the most important and fundamental skills that everybody needs to possess, but only a few are born with it. Students should be taught how to approach people, help them get in touch, how to start a conversation, or talk in a room where no one is talking. All these skills can be taught, and schools should be focusing on this because it's what helps you evolve as a person going forward.

5. **Copywriting**

   Copywriting is the ability to write content that makes people act. Putting your ideas into words and pushing it out in a way that it creates an impact. Copywriting is basic psychology—how a change in wording can change everything for you. And it is a skill that must be taught in school very early on.

6. **Collaborations Are Everything**

   One of the fundamental things that schools can do is organize assignments and competitions for groups rather than solo students. That way, students are able to understand how to work with other people, handle what another person wants with what they want, figure out what is their strength and what their teammates' strengths are. It's a great building exercise for working in a team and together finding a solution to a problem. This will help kids evolve to become good partners later on.

7. **Learning How People Behave and How They Make Decisions**

   Understanding human psychology, what people do and why they do it. Teaching students basic psychology will help them become better humans and make better decisions.

8. **Brand Building**

   People don't buy 'anything', people buy a 'brand'. To build a successful business, you have to build a brand. Why do people want to buy an iPhone instead of a Micromax? How a brand name impacts its business is something that must be taught in school.

9. **Basics of Economics**

   Teaching kids how numbers work, how economics work, basics of economics, savings, investment, etc., is very crucial. Inflation as a topic is something that schools need to teach kids very early on. The biggest problem I have with the education system is that they don't teach kids how money works, and that needs to change.

Eight Things I Wish I Was Taught in School about Social Media and Beyond
By Ranveer Allahbadia (social media entrepreneur)
Instagram: @beerbiceps

1. **Education Degree**

   When I was starting out, people told me I should focus on getting a degree rather than wasting my time on social media. But we live in a modern world and, in this world, we don't necessarily need a higher education to earn a living. Sure, in certain corporate jobs you need formal education, but you can bridge even that gap by self-educating through courses or the internet. Your knowledge is always going to be more valuable than the degree you hold.

2. **Higher Goals Require Bigger Circles**

   Everything grows because of people and never alone. The further you want to go, the bigger your team needs to be. It's something I've thought about a lot. When your goals get higher, the number of people you have to take with you also becomes higher. The game is to find the right mix of people who fit with you. Ideally, don't try to bring your friends into it, instead bring in the people you meet professionally and then turn it into friendship. Business through friendship is bad, but friendship through business is good.

3. **Wellness**

   It is important to focus on your health and wellness. Eating right, exercising, meditating, etc., increases your mental endurance in the long run. The higher the level of your mental endurance, the more you will be able to push forward in life. Your mental endurance is as important as the skills you need to get ahead. You need to inculcate wellness habits from when you are in college itself, and follow them for the rest of your life.

4. **Don't Compromise on Your Sleep**

   If your job is making you compromise on your sleep, either compromise on your job or compromise on your current schedule. Sleep is core to your long-term happiness and performance.

5. **The 3Cs**

   Consistency, compounding and creativity—these are the three pillars that social media stands on. It's the guiding principle to becoming something big on social media. Consistency is the cliché we have all already been told about. Along with that, compounding is equally important. The longer you stay, the faster you will grow.

6. **Video Skills**

   Video skills are something people take for granted. Some people think that, since the future is virtual reality, video skills won't be required much, but the truth is all this is an extension of one skill only, i.e., video editing. The deeper you go into video editing, the more you will grow on social media. Video skills are much more than just editing; it includes storytelling as well. It is something that is both an inherited skill and something you can learn. The inherited part of it is the way you look at your life and your experiences, whereas you can also learn through improving your communication skills.

7. **Delegation Is the Key**

   For me, social media is a creative job. And I think delegation leads to creativity. You need to create a system around you in a way that you are only handling the creative part of the process. I personally don't handle a lot of the business; I have people who do it for me. Every creator should work up to that point where they are only focusing on the creative part of the whole process and not wasting their energy on other things, because I feel like the more energy you save, the more creative you can be. It's not just limited to social media; once you enter any form of entrepreneurship, it's the same rule. The less you have to focus on the operational aspect, the more creative you will be. Delegate everything that takes away your energy and creativity. You don't like looking into finances, delegate it to someone you trust. That's the only reason I have been able to create as much as I have. It takes time to create that system, though.

8. **Focus beyond Social Media**

   Social media is just a stepping stone. It is true for every job in the modern day: you shouldn't stick to just one thing, instead you need to keep thinking what you can do beyond. You need to do something, make it stable, then do something else, make that stable as well, and so on and so forth. What you can do beyond social media is the constant question that you should be asking. You should network with people completely outside of your circle, because they will be able to give you a perspective that you would otherwise miss out on. Your media circle will only give you one kind of input, but your other circles, say finance, will be able to give you a completely different perspective. Apart from that, you should be open to taking intense risks and failing. After three or four failures, you figure out what you're actually built for and have an intense amount of self-discovery through those things. When you are attempting this, you should be financially and mentally at a position where you can afford to fail. Because if you're failing at this, you'd be failing in public, which a lot of people are not ready to do. We should acknowledge that it is okay to fail in public—there's nothing wrong with it. It's just part of the journey.

Seven Things I Wish I Was Taught in School about Becoming a Millionaire
By Raj Shamani
Instagram: @rajshamani

If I was to start from zero, if everything that I have is gone, then how would I start an investment journey to become a millionaire? Read and start taking notes because I'm sure that you will have your investment plan ready by the end of this section.

Whether you are a college-going kid, a person in your thirties or a person starting their investment journey post retirement, you can follow these seven steps to become a millionaire. Those who have thought, 'I want to invest but don't know how to', or those who listened to their friends or somebody on the internet and started investing, but don't know what to do next—this is for you too.

1. **Know Your Money**

   First of all, find out how much money you have. If you get a salary every month then how much is it, or if you have an income then how much is that, or even if you get pocket money then how much is it? Whatever money you get on a monthly basis, note that down and then add your old savings or investments that you have made earlier.

   Once you have done that, make a list of necessary monthly expenses—food, electricity, travel, car, etc. Once you know how much is your income and how much you need to spend, only then will you be able to decide what you want to do next, or how you can start investing.

2. **Set Goals**

   You know how much money you have; now you must be confused about where you should invest. Mutual funds are there, stocks, equity, gold, crypto, so many things . . . WAIT. First of all, figure out *why* do you want to invest?

   You won't be able to reach your destination if you don't know where to go and what is the destination. So, what are your goals? Why do you want to invest? Goals can be anything like to buy a big house, a luxury car, international vacations, education, kids, anything. Write down all your goals and assign a period to each one. Everything must have a time period. For example, I want to retire by the age of forty-five, I want a new car in the next five years, I want to be able to buy a house in the next ten years and go on a vacation to Europe next year. Now, what did I do for every goal? I attached it to a particular timeline. Once you have your goals and a clear vision about timelines, you will be able to choose the right investment options to achieve them. Different plans are suitable for different goals. One type of investment won't achieve all your goals.

3. **Salary and Income Allocation**

   Now, what are salary and income allocation? You know the amount that is coming in, now you need to know where to put that money in order to achieve your goals. This way, a system gets formed and you can also grow an investment discipline. Obviously, it depends from person to person. Everyone has different goals, everyone will have a different salary allocation. You can either think, oh, I will blow up all the money that I have and figure out what happens tomorrow. Or you can think, I'll save today by living a minimal lifestyle, and will live peacefully tomorrow. I would choose living a minimal lifestyle and investing today, so you have a chance of a better tomorrow. Some people will argue, why not live lavishly today, instead of a 'chance' of a better tomorrow, which is uncertain. It's because, as we get older, our energy keeps on decreasing, and our responsibilities increase. So, I usually put 50–70 per cent of my monthly income into investments and only 30 per cent goes towards my living expenses. But when I started, I would put only 10 per cent of my income into investment. It depends where you are starting from. Earlier, I would invest whatever I was left with after travelling, shopping, parties. But then I decided to first invest according to my goals, and after that, whatever was left, I would use for my living expenses. And this helped me grow my net worth significantly.

I would always suggest trying to invest at least 30 per cent of your income, and as you move forward, keep increasing that percentage. Try to keep reducing whatever unnecessary expenses you have and invest that money to achieve your goals faster.

4. **Know Your Risk Appetite**

Risk tolerance is how much of your investment you're willing to lose in order to earn higher returns. Also, what is your goal for that particular investment? For example, let's say you need money for higher education next year. If you need money the next year itself, you won't invest it in high-risk products, because if the market goes down next year, you will lose your money. So, you need to make sure that whatever you have you're putting it as per your risk profile and as per your goals.

How to decide your risk profile? Ask yourself these questions: What is my current financial situation? What responsibilities do I have right now? What do I want to do with this money or what are my goals? Just because a friend is saying invest in crypto, it will increase overnight, doesn't mean you have to invest in that. They might have a different risk profile. Every person's risk profile, goals, financial situation, family condition, family background, everything is different. So, don't do it just because some friend is doing it; look at your situation and then make a decision.

5. **Investment Strategy**

This is the most important part. Now that you know your goals and your risk appetite, it is time to decide on an investment strategy that will help you earn the highest returns possible.

Now, write your long-term goals, medium-term goals and short-term goals on one side of a paper. In the long-term column, write 'high risk', write 'medium risk' in the medium-term goals column, and write 'low risk' in the short-term goals column. Do this right now, on a piece of paper. Your investment strategy should be decided according to this. Your money grows the quickest in high-risk investments, but it also has the highest risk of tanking too. So only invest in high-risk investments when you don't need that money for the next five to ten years. Only then will you be a fruitful investor. High risk, high returns mean US stocks, crypto, and small equity funds.

Now, your medium-risk investments are for when you need money in three to five years. Like blue chip companies, large cap companies, and large cap mutual funds. Your low-risk investments are for when you want the money in a year or two years, like debt funds, government bonds, digital gold, these are comparatively safe and they have less returns too. So, formulate your investment strategy as per the basis of your goals and what you want and your risk analysis. That will also help you stay on track with your investment strategy.

6. **Insurance**

    Life is unpredictable; we don't know which problem will arise when, particularly when it comes to issues related to your health, the life of someone in the family or accidents. I know many people who made great investment plans but had to remove their money because of urgent medical needs, and because of that they were not able to achieve their goals even though they were on the right track. That's why the best way to keep yourself and your family and the money that you have invested safe is to get insurance. And the best age to get insurance is right now. Because the younger you are, the lesser the premium you will have to pay. Generally, one should have at least two types of insurance: life insurance and health insurance.

7. **Diversify Your Investment**

    Now comes one of the most important things—don't keep all your eggs in one basket. Because if anything happens to that basket, then your life's worth of efforts will go in vain. Everything will be gone and all the money earned in your life will also be gone. You all must be thinking that my only goal is to buy a car, why should I diversify? Why not put all my money in one place? NO. Even if you have one goal, don't put all your money in one place. Diversification is very important. You need to invest in two or four or five different kinds of ways to reduce your risk. Because, just like how in life we have good days and bad days, the same way we have bad days in the market as well. And if you have only invested all your money in one thing and there is a bad day, then all of your investment will be gone. But if you put it in different places, one will increase, one will decrease, or while one is decreasing, another is increasing, so all your investments will automatically rise together and sometimes two will increase so rapidly that it will take care of eight other losses.

How would I have started my investment journey if I had to start today? Suppose my income is Rs 50,000 rupees per month, then I would have invested at least 50 per cent of my income in a couple of things. How? Let me tell you. I am twenty-five years old right now and I don't have any family responsibilities. Since I live alone, my expenses are less. So I would have invested Rs 25,000 every month in different things. I'll give you the breakdown. I would have invested 25 per cent in direct equity, small-cap and mutual funds. Since I am investing small amounts, I will do it in mutual funds and small caps because my risk appetite is more at this age. Then I would have invested 25 per cent of my money in index funds. I would have invested another 10 per cent in US stocks mutual funds, because if I am investing less than Rs 2 lakh in US stocks, then I will have a lot of tax problems. So, I will do it in mutual funds that directly invest in US stocks. I would have put 15 per cent into cryptocurrency because I want to and because it has a high-risk high reward.

Then I would have put another 15 per cent in debt funds for emergencies, so that if something bad happens tomorrow then every month my 15 per cent will be secured for emergencies. And then the rest 10 per cent into gold and Exchange Traded Funds (ETFs) for more safety. And that's how I would diversify.

Six Things I Wish I Was Taught in School about Where to Invest
By Raj Shamani
Instagram: @rajshamani

1. **Indian Stock Market**
   You can invest your money in the Indian stock market. If you don't have any idea how to make your investments, you can do it through a portfolio management service (PMS). You need to have Rs 1 crore in order to invest through a PMS. Alternatively, if you don't have that amount, you can invest through smallcase.

2. **American Stock Market**
   The next place you can invest in is the American stock market. If you don't know which companies to invest in, you can go for FAANG: that is, Facebook, Apple, Amazon, Netflix and Google, which are the five most popular and best-performing American tech companies. That is how I started investing in the American stock market.

3. **Early Age Start-ups**
   You can invest in promising start-ups which have the potential to grow tremendously in the future. There's higher risk in investing in early-stage start-ups. But it also promises higher rewards.

4. **Cryptocurrency**

    Cryptocurrencies are all the hype right now. You can start small and, as you keep learning about it, you can keep increasing your investment.

5. **Mutual Funds and Debt Funds**

    There are different kinds of mutual funds. I invest in equity mutual funds which deal in small-caps. Every month, I put a small amount from my portfolio in this through SIP, or Systematic Investment Planning. If you have a lower risk appetite, you can invest in debt funds which have very nominal risks associated with it. You can put a small amount of money in a debt fund, which you can also use as an emergency fund, and take out money whenever you need it.

6. **Others**

    You can invest a small portion of your investment in things which are new or a craze in the West, because by the time they reach India, they'd have grown many times over already. A few such things are NFTs, sneakers, art, wine, etc. I invest a small portion in these fast-growing technologies or ideas, and highly valuable items.

Five Things I Wish I Was Taught in School about Money and Investing
By Rachna Ranade (chartered accountant)
Instagram: @ca_rachanaranade

1. **Savings**

   I think the first thing that should be taught in schools is saving—what is saving, why is it important to save, etc. A lot of kids in school think it's very easy to access money, they don't even understand where money comes from or how much effort is required to earn money. They need to be taught that their parents work every day, day in and day out, and after putting in a lot of effort they get paid for whatever work they do; and that they have to spend from that money and whatever amount is left after that is their savings. If kids are taught at this basic level in school, they will have an understanding of why saving is important and its benefits for a household as a whole. And it is something which can very easily be taught in schools through stories as well.

2. **Insurance**

   Just saving isn't enough. Kids need to be taught how they can protect the money they have saved as well. Even this can be easily taught in a story format. Suppose you have something which is very valuable to you, let's say, an iPhone. Someone comes to you and tells you that if you pay Rs 2000 to them now, they are going to protect your iPhone for the next two years. That is, if anything happens to your phone—

it breaks or gets stolen—they'll give you another iPhone. Now, if nothing happens, he'll still keep that Rs 2000. That person is the insurer, the amount you paid is called premium, and the service you're getting is insurance.

3. **Taxes**

   Students should be introduced to the basics of taxes, like what are direct taxes, indirect taxes and GST. They should be taught the importance of taxes and why people have to pay taxes. Once we grow up, it's all about how to save taxes, but it should be taught why the country needs tax collection, how we are contributing to a bigger cause by paying these taxes, how the government needs money to spend on infrastructure and how it in turns help us as citizens. We should feel happy while paying taxes—we are contributing towards the success of the economy.

4. **Investment**

   The first thing that needs to be taught about investment is the risk-return pyramid. Imagine a pyramid. The base of the pyramid is where the risk is the lowest and also the return is the lowest; the more we move towards the tip of the pyramid, the more the risk and the return on the investment increases. Fixed deposits with nationalized banks, post office schemes, etc., come at the bottom of the pyramid. Above it would be mutual funds, then above that would be equity, above that would be crypto, above that would be collectibles or NFTs. If this pyramid is taught in school, people will know which asset class has the highest risk and which has the lowest. Everyone should do their risk profiling according to their risk appetite. People who can't take risks should invest in fixed deposits; people who have a high-risk appetite can go for NFTs, etc.

5. **Basic Financial Knowledge**

   Many people don't even have basic financial knowledge, like how to open a bank account, what's the difference between a debit card and a credit card, etc. There's an emerging concept of pay-later cards, which should also be taught in school. Many people don't know the importance of having a nominee to their account. People should also be taught that when they keep money in their savings' account, up to Rs 5 lakh is insured by the Deposit Insurance Credit Guarantee Corporation (DICGC), which means that if you have a savings' account in a co-operative bank, and that bank goes insolvent, up to Rs 5 lakh of your account is safe. It's surprising that so many people don't even know these things; it's important that they should be taught in school.

Four Things I Wish I Was Taught in School About life
By Masoom Minawala Mehta (entrepreneur)
Instagram: @masoomminawala

1. **How to Pay My Taxes**

   School didn't teach us anything about paying our taxes. It is something we all have to do, irrespective of our fields. Paying your taxes is a skill we are assumed to learn on the job or we have to trust someone else with it. It is not a financial skill, it is a life skill. Schools should teach us the process and procedure of paying our taxes because, at the end of the day, we end up paying taxes in one form or another.

2. **It's Okay to Fail**

I wish I had been taught in school that failing is completely okay. It's not spoken about enough, and it's not normalized enough. In a given twenty-four hours, we encounter so many failures, whether big or small—as an entrepreneur, we are failing at least three to four times a day, whether it is in the form of disappointments or rejections. How we should react to them and how we should respond to them is something I wish I had been taught. Failure is not about one devastating moment, it is more about everyday moments. We need to normalize failure because, no matter what you do, if you are trying to grow, you're going to fail more times than you're probably going to achieve success.

So many stories that we are taught in school are success driven. If failure could also be celebrated in that way, imagine how fulfilling life could actually be. The thing we should be celebrating is our efforts and the process.

3. **Time Management**

Time management is the most important life skill that one can have. If you know how to manage your time better, you can have a four-hour working day and achieve as much as you would in a ten-hour working day. Time management is a skill which should be taught in school like algebra, because it is the solution to living a balanced and fulfilling life.

4. **Networking**

Networking is a skill which you need in your day-to-day life. Schools don't teach us how to network. People complicate networking as well. You know someone, who knows someone, who knows someone else—this chain is basically called networking. Now, how can you do that? More often than not, networking is done with the intention of getting to know someone instead of having an end goal in mind. You need to identify people you would be interested in knowing. After that, all you need to do is know how to make conversation. And how can you make conversation? By talking about something that the other person would want to engage in. Find common ground—it could be anything that interests both of you—and ask questions that the other person would want to answer. By the end of the conversation, you would know someone who would know twenty other people who would know fifty other people who could help you in the future.

Three Things I Wish I Was Taught In School about Making Money
By Nikhil Kamath (entrepreneur)
Instagram: @nikhilkamathcio

They don't teach you anything about making money in school—that is the whole problem.

1. **Timing Is Everything**

    The first thing school fails to teach us is that timing is everything. What you do when determines how well you do it—for example, what business you should start and when. If you're graduating from college today, are you going to start a business which is working now or a business which will be relevant in the next decade? Choosing the right industry and right job at the right time is very important. How can you do that? When you are out of school, what do you do to find the right course or college for yourself? You research. And that's what you need to do here too.

2. **Have a Side Hustle**

    Your side hustle doesn't have to start when you're grown up. Start looking for opportunities when you are in college instead of when you have graduated and have to work. Having a side hustle early in life teaches you a lot. It teaches you how to work in a team, how to build a product together, money management, and the discipline required to keep a job. Americans have this culture and we need to adopt it too.

3. **Teach Finance in a Pragmatic Manner**
    What school teaches us about finance is outdated and irrelevant. Schools need to teach finance in a more pragmatic manner. More practical and real-time financial knowledge will help people manage their money better when they eventually start earning. Schools should teach the importance of diversification, the different asset classes, what are some of the things that people who have done something in their lives did with their money, and the like. Finance is not as complicated as people make it appear. What school teaches us is the history of finance and the Indian banking system, which is irrelevant. Instead, it should focus on more relevant aspects like which investment worked in which era and why.

Two Essentials of Life I Wish I Was Taught in School
By Ashok Ramachandran (CEO / President, Schindler India)
Instagram: @ramachandranash

1. **Mindfulness and Focus**
    Mindfulness is the ability of being present in the moment. 'Keep your mind where your hands are'—we have all heard this age-old saying. It means you should only pay attention to what you are doing at a particular moment. The point of 'eating what you are eating' is not the eating but developing focus. When you're fully engrossed in the one thing that you are doing, you develop focus. How does this help, though? It helps you

when you actually need to focus on something. You'll be able to focus when you keep practising it every day.

2. **How to Be Disciplined**

   You don't have to wait for some major event to happen in your life in order to do the right things. Discipline comes from doing the right things. And you do the right things when you have bigger goals in mind. Discipline comes from having good habits. Having a good set of people around you also helps you to be more disciplined.

One Thing I Wish I Was Taught in School
By Raj Shamani
Instagram: @rajshamani

One thing school doesn't teach us is how to figure out things. They tell us a set path to follow, and a way to learn and do things. Schools never teach us how to get stuff done either; we should be taught how to make things happen. Schools should become more practical and less theoretical. Instead of making us repeat what we crammed from a sheet of paper, schools need to help us figure out things for ourselves.

Printed in Great Britain
by Amazon

46689504R00128